A Woman's Ransom

A WOMAN'S RANSOM.

VOL. III.

A WOMAN'S RANSOM.

BY

FREDERICK WILLIAM ROBINSON,

AUTHOR OF

"GRANDMOTHER'S MONEY," "UNDER THE SPELL,"
"WILDFLOWER," "SLAVES OF THE RING,"
&c., &c.

"Who sows the serpent's teeth, let him not hope
To reap a joyous harvest. Every crime
Has, in the moment of its perpetration,
Its own avenging angel."
SCHILLER.

IN THREE VOLUMES.
VOL. III.

LONDON:
HURST AND BLACKETT, PUBLISHERS,
SUCCESSORS TO HENRY COLBURN,
13, GREAT MARLBOROUGH STREET.
1864.
The right of Translation is reserved.

250. p. 96.

LONDON:
PRINTED BY MACDONALD AND TUGWELL, BLENHEIM HOUSE,
BLENHEIM STREET, OXFORD STREET.

CONTENTS

OF

THE THIRD VOLUME.

———

CONTENTS.

BOOK V.

CONTINUED.

IN THE MISTS.

" All do so like saints appear,
  We know not who's a devil here."
                              CANIDIA, 1683.

" *Exupere.* L'apparence vous trompe, et je suis en effet—
Léontine. L'homme le plus mêchant que la nature ait fait."
                              CORNEILLE.

A WOMAN'S RANSOM.

CHAPTER XIII.

THE PAST.

It had flashed across me in the dim uncertainty; it had been whispered in the turmoil of action following Ellen's disappearance; in the midst of other fears that great and ghastly one had come without an effort of my own, and kept a place beside me. I had tried to live it down; I had thought to keep it at arm's length, amongst the intangibilities which encompass a man, unable to stir hand or foot, and yet pining to act for one in tribulation.

In my heart, with all the facts against her, I had thought it more probable that Ellen should die, or

seek death, rather than she should fly to shame
for solace.   More than once I had prayed that she
might be dead, rather than the partner of guilt
with Wenford.

And yet, thinking and praying thus at uncertain intervals, I could not keep a host of thoughts
from pressing closer to my reason—a phalanx that
destroyed the wilder theory of Ellen's innocence,
and left a portion of her shame with me.

When my wife had given vent to her own suspicions, a sudden revulsion seized me in the first
icy moments following her avowal.   Ellen's guilty
flight with Wenford, a trampling under foot of
God's laws, and her own purity and honour—all
better than a death sudden and unprepared for, a
coward's blow struck at her in the dark.

" You think that she is dead then, Mary?"

" Yes," she answered.

" You will tell me why you think so?" I said,
" ever from to-night no half confidences between
us?"

" Canute, I will tell you all."

She nestled closer to me for that protection
which she felt was nearer when my arms were
round her—as though she feared her own life
might pay the penalty of her confession.   Her

voice trembled very much at first, but gathered strength as she became excited, and rang out at last with the unfaltering accents of an indignant woman.

"Canute, I believe that she is dead. In all my life I have not known a woman less likely to abjure her marriage vows, and fly the shelter of her husband's home. I believe it for two reasons: first, that her death would leave my brother free; secondly, because with that brother has ever been a lust for gold so intense and unnatural as to sweep aside *by any means* all obstacles that barred his way to wealth. Years ago when I trusted him more and feared him less, he sold his soul for money!"

"He may be a covetous man, Mary—I have known more than one—but surely there would be barriers drawn by God's hand in his path, and he would pause before them."

"Did I think so when you found me at his feet the morning after Ellen's disappearance?" she said; "on that day I knelt to him, and implored him, for his own sake, to tell me where Ellen was. To all his story of her flight, of his despair, of Wenford's treachery, I asked where Ellen was, until he cursed me for a madwoman."

" Strange that you should doubt him more than I."

" I have seen the mask drop," she said in an excited whisper; " against my own trust in his worthiness, has forced slowly its way the one great truth of his gigantic villainy. There, I have said it—I have owned it to you, as I owned it once to Janet years ago."

" And Janet—"

" Believes in him still—will set all down to the morbid fancies which have distressed me many years. All this to comfort me perhaps, to shut her eyes against the wickedness of him whom she has loved from his cradle-side."

" But Ellen's letter—Wenford's letter ?"

" I must speak more of them presently," she said with a shudder, " of my reasons for believing them forgeries. Oh! Canute," she cried passionately, " I am sacrificing Herbert for my husband's love—I who thought to die with never a word against him to escape me."

· " Words will not injure him, and if he be all that you suspect, for Ellen's sake, to afford a clue to my unhappy sister's disappearance, for the sake of honour, justice, even the lives of others, you have a right to speak."

"I think so," said she, gathering courage; "now listen to me, and tell me if I have been suspicious all my life—if in my heart I have wronged him. Years ago, Janet told me that I understood him not, that my own nervous fancies conjured up horrors which had no real foundation—that for some actions of his own, which were not to be excused, I never made sufficient allowance—that all my life I have played a cruel part towards him. If you will think so too, I shall be ever after this the happiest of women!"

She paused, and raised her head from my shoulder to look steadily across the room, with one white hand pressed to her bosom, as though the phantoms of the past were ranging themselves before her, and she had scarcely found courage to face them at the last. The past was a grim retrospect, but she went upon her backward way for my sake and for Ellen's.

"Let me hurry on my story," she began; "I need not dwell upon my single life, scarcely on my married. You know that Mr. Zitman returned to his native place a wealthy man; a man much older than myself, a hard stern being, with that love of money ingrained in him which we have seen in his sister, Mrs. Ray. He was a rich man, who sought my father's house, who, after a while, made it almost his home, who eventually asked me to become his wife. To that marriage step by step, forced forwards as it were by my father and my brother, I was led. They made my home wretched, my life miserable, and I married Mr. Zitman to escape them, God forgive me!"

"Why dwell on this?" I said. "Why do I sit here listening to this—to you who are not so strong and well as I could wish yet? To-morrow——"

"I am strong enough," she interrupted, "I am going through my task now, bravely and fearlessly. The guilt of my long silence is oppressive, and I must have your old love back, your old trust and confidence in me. Mr. Zitman did not make me happy—after my father's death, when my brother, to whom he had taken a fancy, was living under the same roof with us, I was less happy still—I was watched, mistrusted, treated as a cypher in the house to which I had been lured. In that house, I first suspected Herbert. He played a double part—professing friendship and love to both, and yet setting one against the other, surely and insidiously. To me, he spoke much of the advantages accruing from the death of my husband—of

my young widowhood, and the days of freedom
that would follow it—he played the tempter till I
bade him silence, and shut my ears for ever
against the cruel ideas which he had given birth
to. At this time my husband went to London on
business with my brother—he left in good health
and strength; and *he died within the week!*"

"But——"

"Patience, patience!" she cried; "all is suspicion—there are no facts—I cannot reason! I discovered, afterwards, that a day or two before his
death, Herbert had forged my husband's name to
a cheque for two thousand pounds, and that discovery was imminent—I know that he returned
triumphantly to Nettlewood, to congratulate me
on my liberty, and to eventually exercise over me
a tyranny greater than my married life had
witnessed. Still, even then, I did not think him
the murderer of my husband, until I found how
deep a schemer every action proved him. There
came a time when Wenford sought to marry me—
I believed that man loved me after his wild fashion,
and that over his better nature I had some influence then, though I dared not trust my future
with him, though I never dreamed of loving him.
My brother wished that marriage—threatened me

if I rejected him, made my home a house of
bondage, in the hope that I should leap towards
Wenford for escape, used every means, every cruel
artifice, to make me call that man my husband."

"Was this reasonable?"

"The money would have passed to the Rays,
and he was professing love to Letty Ray at that
time—if I had married Wenford, Letty would
have been his wife within the week. They were
whispering in the village of his attentions to the
girl, when I told Wenford it was beyond my
power to love him. And then——"

She paused, with her face more ashen still, with
a look upon it that made me fear for her, and
accuse myself for listening thus so patiently, and
yet which held me by a spell that was irresistible
to break through.

"And then he schemed for my life—to cast
me down by my own nervous fears, or failing
that, *to poison me*."

"This can't be, Mary. He was never so great
a villain—this must have been a delusion."

"They tried to make it appear so, when I was
on my guard—when I had confessed my fears to
Janet, and Janet had affected to laugh at them.
I believed, then, that my husband had died by

Herbert's hands—and that my life was unsafe, if
he thought of marrying Letty Ray. I knew that
he was a forger—that he had forged my name
since my husband's death—that whenever he required money he signed my name in the cheque-
book, and relied upon his sister's pride to shield
him—I knew that we had quarrelled, and I had
warned him of his crimes—I knew that he was
dangerous, and had no mercy on those who kept
him down. Janet—my own trusty watcher—
would not hear of my suspicions, and laughed at
them before me. But, Canute, I was watching in
my turn then, and in the library I heard, once,
Janet and my brother at high words. She was
taking my part then—she warned him that if he
thought or dreamed of evil, she would denounce
him if I came to harm—she spoke of her
love for him, her hope in him yet, her doubts
if all that I suspected could be true, but she told
him that he was mistrusted, and—I think she
saved my life! Poor Janet, she will ever think
the best of him through all—she believes in him
yet, though his own sister has lost all love and
faith."

"A hundred suspicions float above us both, but
there is nothing tangible to grasp at. Devoid of

principle, a forger and a villain, still there is no proof of darker, deeper crimes."

"Those doubts were the faint gleams of light upon the path before I met with you," she said, "they crossed the darker ones, and kept me wholly from despair—at times, I tried my best to believe in them."

"Is there anything more to say, Mary?"

"Only this, that my fear of him became more intense as I grew weaker; that, in striving to think my past suspicions the faint shadows of a dream, I felt my reason giving way, and right and wrong becoming inextricably confused. My one hope was to live apart from him—hence the scheme for a new house, wherein I could feel safe from harm. By that time I had assured him that I should never marry, that I would be content to live away from him, and allow him an annual income which would satisfy even his rapacity, and on those terms he was content to let me go—nay, glad to part with me. I did not know then what was coming from the distance to make my life a brighter one—I did not believe in any one sacrificing all for me, and loving me for my own wilful self."

"You had lived in an enervating atmosphere, and lost all confidence in honest hearts," I said, pressing her closer to me. "At least, this is a brighter time for you."

"It was, until I feared that your love was fading away also."

"Never that. I was disturbed concerning the grim past which haunted you—nothing more, my Mary."

"It is an awful past—judge how it has affected one ever weak and delicate. Is there anything more to say, Canute?" she asked, "of the competition scheme—of my brother's wish to constitute you the architect—of his search for you in London —of his own attraction towards your sister—an attraction that might have saved him and moulded his character anew, if love of money could have been set further from his heart. Canute, I believe for a time he *did* love her—until she read his sordid nature, as I had read it in the years before she met him. When he was married to her, he heard for the first time of my intention to become your wife; you remember how he hurried back here whilst you were in London—that he might work upon my fears, and my old promise to him, to break off the engagement we had formed. But, oh, Canute! your love had made me strong, and I could not regret the first promise which I had ever broken in my life, when the fairer days before me were making even the present bearable. When I stood my ground, he changed his, and perpetrated one more forgery, which made Nettlewood House his own. For Ellen's sake, I let the veil drop over his last struggle for a portion of the riches that were melting from me ; and I passed from the wild life of uncertainty with him to peace and rest with you."

It was a wild story, built up of fancies and suspicions, yet verging on an awful truth. Tortured by these fancies, seeing the lowness and the craftiness of the man with whom her life had been spent, I could believe how much her mind had borne, and wonder that it had not given way more utterly. I could believe, too, in these fancies—in the depths of that stern character which knew no law save its own awful passions. This man was no common villain—he was a clever man who having made CRIME his study, had become a professor in the art. Such men had lived to shame humanity, and shock it by a felon's death. Here and there, in the grim calendar of prison annals, such men stalked, for honest folk to wonder at. He was a man trebly dangerous, for the few signs he made—every action of his life was part and parcel of some scheme which threatened evil to his victims.

"You are silent, Canute," she said; "will you tell me, if, knowing him to be a villain in one respect, I have judged him too harshly and severely in another—if I have ungenerously believed the very worst of him?"

"All is dark before us—but we will not judge him yet awhile."

"But you fear—you doubt?"

"I fear for Ellen more than ever, Mary," I said. "I must find out, for her sake and my own, what has become of her."

"Yes—it must be," murmured Mary.

"This man, if he be innocent, will thank me for following the mystery to the end; if he be guilty, and would screen his guilt by blasting the fair fame of his victim, he is not worthy of your pity, and is *too dangerous to live!*"

"No—no—you will have mercy on him at the last, Canute," she said, "for the sake of Ellen, you will not forget your wife."

"Ellen's last words were that 'the mists were closing round her.' I must fight my way through

them to her—or her grave. When the broad
light is upon us all again, we will think of what
mercy to mete out to that man."

I had no thought of mercy then, but my wife's
wild looks warned me to hide the bitter longing I
felt to hunt Vaughan to the death. And with
the mists around us all, what right had I to assume
the avenger's part so soon?

"I must stay a little while longer in Nettlewood,
Mary—once again postpone my return to Borrowdale. But you, if you love me, will go back and
make my mother's house your home, for the few
days that I shall be away from you."

"You are going into danger?"

"No—I trust not."

"For my sake, you will be careful not to make
my brother Herbert your enemy. Promise me that,
and that you will not be very long away, and I
shall have courage to part with you—if it be
necessary."

"There is a stern necessity to act, and I cannot
avoid it."

I had made up my mind in what way to proceed,
but I spared my wife an outline of my plans.
When she was away, *when she was more safe*, I
would make my first step into the shadow-land

wherein poor Ellen had vanished. Then, step by step to the end, swerving not to right or left until I found her in her shame, or in her grave—to pity or avenge her.

There must have been signs of this set determination in my looks, for Mary's arms were round my neck again, and she whispered,

"You will think of me—you will not forget me, Canute?"

"Never."

"I fear now," she said, irresolutely, "that I have done wrong—that in my selfish wish to have no clouds between us, I have confessed too much, and spoken too much against him. My doubts steal back—my old belief in him returns."

"I have said we will not judge him yet, Mary."

At this moment the Ferry bell across the river clanged loudly—some one was anxious to reach Nettlewood.

"He has come back again," said Mary.

I drew the blind aside, and looked out into the dark night. Jabez and his man were tramping about with lanterns in their hands. I opened the window, and called out,

"Who's coming to Nettlewood, Jabez?"

"Measter Vaughan, I think. Do you wish to see him?"

"No—not now."

I did not draw the blind across the window, but remained there—Mary came and linked her hands upon my arm, to watch there also. We were both silent—it was a dark night, with few stars shimmering above where the secrets of all hearts were known.

Across the water in the large ferry-boat, came Vaughan at last, his hand upon the bridle of his horse, as I had seen him once before.

For the first time in my life I had watched him come towards me, as he came now. I had other hopes then; life was different with me; Ellen was a governess at home; Mary Zitman I had seen but once; life had not been turned suddenly from its silent course into a vortex of romance.

The words of Mrs. Ray came back to me, wild and ominous as though they were ringing from her grave in Henlock churchyard.

"He is coming at us like a Fate!"

And on he came that night again, "to pass by us unacknowledged"—the Fate that had shadowed his sister's life and mine, and left Ellen's hard to guess at—the Fate that I was gathering strength to cope

with! In the dim future stretched the battle-
ground wherein he and I should meet—was Ellen
lying there already, with her face upturned to the
heaven that had been so pitiless?

END OF BOOK V.

BOOK VI.

IN SEARCH.

" Lucius, the torrent bears too hard upon me :
Justice gives way to force."

ADDISON.

" I charge thee, keep this secret close."

OTWAY.

CHAPTER I.

THE FIRST STEP.

WHEN Mary had returned to Borrowdale, I began the task, which, but for Mary's illness, I should have commenced a month ago. There was a clue to find, failing which I might return home on the morrow—discovering which might lead me many miles away. Mary took back with her a letter of mine to Mr. Sanderson, explaining my future intentions, craving his indulgence as a partner and friend, if, for a short while, business were neglected by me. To that faithful friend I confessed my utter inability to work, and dwelt upon the fever that was consuming me to know more of her who had been spirited away. From him, in due course, I received an answer—kind and fatherly, containing much shrewd advice not to be led too far, but wishing me, as I knew he would, God speed in the task I had set myself. He thought—or rather his letter conveyed the impression—that I was full of the one hope to rescue Ellen from further sin, to test her sister's love for me by urging her to give up him who had seduced her from her home; he did not know the darker shades which the story had taken since he had heard it first, or the belief that in my heart was strengthening so fast.

Fortunately I had a good excuse for lingering in Nettlewood—the library alterations were being proceeded with again; the stately heiress to her mother's possessions was anxious that all her mother's wishes should be carried out to the letter. Of that heiress I saw little; she flitted before me once or twice in her deep mourning, and seemed always anxious to avoid a conversation; when we were compelled to meet, she spoke alone of business, and appeared ever solicitous to curtail her interviews. With her new possessions she had entered into a new reserve that was chilling, almost repulsive; she was the lady patroness

now, and I was her inferior, to be treated with
cold politeness, nothing more. The old times had
vanished too far back for me to intrude upon her
companionship, or claim to be her friend—or else
those fragments of her mother's story which had
oozed out at the inquest, had rendered her reluctant to face one who was a representative of her
strange sad past.

For these reasons, or others for which I did not
care to seek a solution, Letty Ray held herself
aloof from me. This did not disturb me, or arouse
my curiosity for a while—I had but one idea, and
that possessed me utterly. On the first night that
I was left alone in Nettlewood, I locked the door
upon my reverie, and held silent communion with
my thoughts. Until all facts were ranged calmly
and methodically side by side, and I could trace,
as it were upon a map, the progress of the story,
till it ended abruptly like a ruin, I was powerless
to act.

On the evening of the 20th of July, I saw my
sister for the last time; she was troubled then,
troubled at her husband's attention to Miss Ray,
and unsettled at a something looming indistinctly
in the background. Did she fear for her life then?
Across her startled fears was there flung, at that

time, the shadow of the danger which approached her—leaving there, did that danger suddenly and swiftly fall upon her before escape was possible? If that were true, Janet could tell me, perhaps—Janet, who was in the house that night. If all that Vaughan had told me were true, there would be no difficulty in ascertaining if Mr. Wenford made preparations for flight, and if they fled away together. That last task I set myself in the first instance.

The ground was easy to work upon—a servant or two of Mr. Wenford's household were accustomed to stray down to the tap-room of the Ferry Inn, to gossip on Nettlewood matters over a mug of Jabez's ale—since Mr. Wenford's departure to appear more frequently, even smoke and drink away the day there, like servants neglectful of a house deserted by its master. More than once lately I had heard them grumbling over the hard times which left their salaries unpaid, and themselves irresolute how to proceed, and had passed them by unheeded—that day, after my wife's departure, when one of the grooms was smoking his pipe at the table on the grass-plot, I strolled from the inn towards him.

I had become well known to all Nettlewood

folk by this time, and his "good day, Mr. Gear," was nothing new or strange.

"What! here again?" I ventured to remark, in the first instance.

The man was full of his wrongs, and resented my observation at once.

"What does it matter where I am, sir?—there's no one to order me now the master's away, and the house is going to the dogs. Like the butler, and the coachman, and the cook, I'm waiting for my wages."

"How will you get them?"

"The creditors are down upon the place. The Larches is to be sold somewhere in London—we shall be paid out of the estate."

"And the horses?"

"Oh! they'll go with the rest, barring the one Mr. Wenford rode away on, and the one he lent Jem Baines."

"Did Baines accompany your master, then?"

"Yes. Odd to pick upon that fellow who was discharged for impudence to Mr. Vaughan, wasn't it, sir? And I was always master's favourite man —he couldn't do nothing without me once. If it hadn't a-been for that Jem Baines, I should have been along with the guv'nor in furrin parts, where

he's spending his money with the lady who—oh !
I beg your pardon, sir. I forgot, you see."

The man reddened and looked confused. I told
him there was nothing to beg my pardon about;
and, fearful of arousing his suspicions by further
inquiries, I left him to his pipe and ale in the sunshine. I strolled along the banks of the lake to ponder on the result of my first step—from it had
evolved more than I had dreamed of, more than I
could see the reason for.

I had learned at least that James Baines—the
past tool of Mrs. Ray—had accompanied Mad
Wenford, and that both had left on horseback.
The thought struck me then that perhaps Ellen *had*
fled with Wenford, that James Baines was an accomplice and had assisted in her flight, placing his
horse at the disposal of Mrs. Vaughan when she
had passed from her husband's home. I tried to
recollect at what hour Wenford had left Mrs. Ray's
house, and recalled his strange demeanour when
he stood at the door of the supper-room, and spoke
of business taking him away. I remembered a gilt
time-piece on the mantel-shelf chiming twelve; if
he, taking advantage of Vaughan's presence at the
supper-table, had seized that opportunity to set off
with my sister, they would have reached Henlock

before one. They would not have stopped at Henlock for an instant, but have gone on down the vale, or over the bridge at the base of the Black Gap range of mountains. Down the vale there was no village for a good fourteen miles—across the bridge and taking the car road, long and circuitous, to Borrowdale, there were only a few houses dotting the road here and there, and, I believe, no place where it was likely they could have halted and refreshed or changed their horses. In all probability they would have proceeded down the Vale of Nettlewood, as far as Horley—the village already mentioned—changed horses, and gone on again. They would have reached Horley about four, and, in the dead hours of the night, must have aroused some one or other to attend to them. I would try Horley first, at least.

I set off on my fourteen miles' walk that afternoon, and reached Horley at seven in the evening.

Horley was a straggling but large village, chiefly peopled by miners, who worked at some lead mines in the district. There were two inns to Horley, and one beer-shop on the outskirts of the town beyond Horley. Surely, if there were a lady and gentleman riding through here at four in the morning they would have been seen, and their horses must have been fatigued sufficiently to require some degree of attention.

I proceeded to the inns forthwith, where no news awaited me. Mad Wenford was well known to both the landlords; if he had aroused them in the early morning of the twenty-first of July, they would not have forgotten it very soon. They knew Mad Wenford—they had heard the new story connected with his name, and their memory was not likely to betray them in this instance. The landlord of the "Crown" only remembered being aroused once in the night in all his life, and that was in the old coaching days, when there was a break down in the High Street. I went on to the beer-shop, and received no information there. Tired and dispirited, I walked back into the town, to the first inn where I had made inquiry concerning the fugitives.

I called for a mug of ale there, and took my place in a corner of the bar-parlour, and waited for the landlord's evening customers. After a while one or two straggled in: the butcher of the town for his evening glass of gin and water, and the ubiquitous parish-clerk, who haunts the parlours of all inns, country and town, and takes the easy chair and corner place.

Casually I asked of them if they remembered the twenty-first of July, or the night of the twentieth, and they stared vacantly at me, the parish-clerk asking me why I put the question to them? I informed them that I was anxious to ascertain whether any person, or persons, rode through the town whilst its inhabitants were sleeping; and the parish-clerk fancied that he was woke up out of his sleep one night in the summer, but dashed if he knew when or by what. I was a detective policeman after some one, perhaps, he asked inquisitively, and seemed disappointed when I responded in the negative.

It was his turn to put questions to me, but I balked them by snatching at a newspaper, and applying myself to its contents.

It was a Cumberland newspaper, two weeks old, and contained some scraps of local news, and a plethoric array of advertisements, directing attention to sales, and recommending quack medicines, which people had long since grown tired of in London.

By way of refuge, I was studying these advertisements, when one leaped, as it were, towards me, and startled me by its appeal to the facts I was anxious to arrive at. I had to take a firmer grasp of the newspaper to conceal the evidence of my hand shaking from the two men quietly smoking their pipes at a little distance from me. I read carefully the advertisement twice. It ran as follows :

"NOTICE.—If the parties who left two horses at Quirkett's Farm, near Horley, on the morning of the twenty-first of July last, do not fetch or send for the same, on or before the fourteenth of August next ensuing, they will be sold to pay expenses."

"Where's Quirkett's Farm ? " I asked, throwing down the paper, and leaping to my feet.

" Three miles from here, I should say," said the butcher, " further down the Vale. You know the Triesdale Pass, mayhap ? "

" No."

" It's close agin it—that's all."

" Thank you."

I went out of the room with my heart beating somewhat faster. The parish-clerk slapped his hand upon his knee as I went out.

"That man's after some poor fellow, I'll lay sixpence. He's sharp-set on to something."

I went through the town, and past the beer-shop again. I set forth at a smart pace towárds

Quirkett's Farm—the excitement of pursuit was making my blood warm. The chase had begun, and I was entering upon it with all that energy which more than once in life had startled those who had seen me roused to action. It was a gift of God's, that perseverance under difficulties, and I thanked Him for it then. I felt that I should never give way until the end was reached, or death met me by the way.

There was no difficulty in discovering Quirkett's Farm—a low, old-fashioned, heavily-thatched building, standing at the opening to one of those wild, picturesque mountain passes in which Cumberland abounds. A gloomy scene it presented, in the twilight, with the silence of the dead around me.

I toiled up the hill towards the farm, and knocked at the stout oaken door, with the handle of my walking-cane; a short burly man, with a red face and sandy whiskers, responded to my summons.

" Your name is Quirkett ? "

" The tother man who deed here wor, not me."

" This is Quirkett's Farm, at least ? "

" Ay."

" In the early morning of the twenty-first of July last two horses were left here ? "

"Dorm their blood!—t'eat their heads off—yes."

"Are the horses here?"

"I ha' soold 'em. I said I would — I'll tak' the reesponsibilitee — do your worst!" he shouted.

"I don't want the horses—I only wish to know why they were left here at all?"

"One had goon lame, and the other had been stooned by so many coots over the head with the boot end· of a wheep—the tall mad fellow did that."

"A man and woman brought those horses?"

"No—two men."

"One a groom?"

"Ay—I theenk so—I moind some white bootins sheening in the candle-light."

"And the other a very tall man, with thick moustaches—Wenford of Nettlewood."

"I'm a new coomer, and doan't knoo Wenford of Nettlewood— and doan't woan't to knoo. Tall he wor, with mustaches like a Chaneyman. I'm oot o' pocket by these horses—ha' ye coom to pay the deeference?"

"Which way did those men go after leaving here?" I asked.

"Up the pass. Ha' ye coom——"

"Can the pass lead towards Nettlewood, or join any mountain track from Nettlewood?"

"It leads bang away to Raverdale, and I doan't knoo anything o' Nettlewood. I've told ye so—ha' ye coom to pay the difference, now?"

"I have not," I answered; "I am in search of those two men—I am anxious to reach Raverdale to-night. How far is it?"

"Sax miles by the pass. I've a mule I can let out for sax-and-saxpence, and my boy'll guide ye for half-a-croon. He's a mighty deal o' help to the towrists that are always bothering aboot here."

"I'll have the mule."

Waiting for the mule, I conversed still further with the owner of the farm, who, despite his bombast, appeared to me somewhat relieved in mind that I had not called to claim the horses, or argue upon the difference between their keep and the product derived from their sale. I learned from him that master and groom went down the pass on foot, the master swearing volubly all the time that he was within hearing. Feeling convinced that all clue to Ellen was lost in this direction, I yet went on to Raverdale, reaching there at ten in

D 2

the evening, when the houses of the early villagers were closed. A small village, with only one inn—the landlady a voluble being with an excellent memory, that treasured up every incident · which had happened in her experience within the last five and forty years. She remembered the 21st of July well—the early hour at which a groom entered the inn, and had a flask filled with brandy,, whilst the other man, a very tall one, passed through the village without looking right or left. She fancied it was Mr. Wenford, of whom she had heard many times, but she had only seen him once, and couldn't swear to him. Both men were very muddy about the legs, and no doubt had come from Horley by the Triesdale Pass. I slept at the inn that night, resolving to hasten back in the early morning to Nettlewood again.

I went at once to my room, to escape half a dozen boisterous tourists, who were making the parlour ring with their hearty English merriment.

Thinking over the incidents of that day, and of the result of the first step in search of Ellen, my impulse was to feel grateful that she had not fled with Wenford. Unless I had been wholly deceived, and had followed a false track, which seemed impossible, I was at least spared the shame of discovering that Ellen was unworthy of further search. Better dead than to have discovered that!

My heart sank fearfully at this thought an instant afterwards. Better dead in her youth and beauty, when life should be opening to her fair and radiant—dead by the coward's hand that struck at her when she feared no evil!

Herbert Vaughan had told me at the Ferry Inn that she had fled with Wenford. Why did he tell me that lie?—why did I feel that night, though baffled in my search, so near unto the truth he had striven so desperately to hide from me?

CHAPTER II.

JANET'S DEFENCE.

FROM the Triesdale Pass to Nettlewood there was
no track, the landlady told me in the morning;
she had heard of a man making a path for himself across the mountains, but no one believed
the story, inasmuch as there were two ranges of
hills between Triesdale and Nettlewood, and like-
wise a rugged gap to cross. It might be just
possible, but there would be a losing of time and
a considerable amount of extra fatigue.

In her new home, Ellen had taken a fancy for
long mountain rambles, but it was not probable, I
thought, that if she had left in the night's darkness,

she would have attempted so impracticable a way, or have chosen that route at all, even to meet the man with whom it was supposed that she had fled.

I gave up the idea of that guilty flight at once. I had tracked Wenford to Raverdale; there seemed no possibility of Ellen meeting him, or a reason for meeting him there, when it was far more easy to have accompanied him at once. I set aside Wenford's departure as something separate and distinct from Ellen's disappearance. Possibly it had been planned to occur at the same time by the master schemer who had worked the mystery, and, failing other means, I might yet be forced to follow the old track and discover Wenford's whereabouts. Something more concerning the troubles of that night Wenford was aware of; he and Vaughan had plotted together for years, though Wenford might be but the tool for more skilful hands to work with.

I thought of my first journey from London, and my first meeting with Wenford; there recurred to me again the scene by the Windermere lake and the two figures on the bench by the lake's margin. I felt convinced now that they were Vaughan and Wenford, and that the latter had been sent to spy upon me, to gain some further clue to my character, perhaps, ere I was inducted into my post as architect to Mrs. Zitman.

It might be necessary to endeavour to find Wenford presently. I had at that time discovered sufficient for my purpose—Ellen had not fled with him. I started at an early hour for Nettlewood again, and reached the old scene of action early in the afternoon. I walked my twenty miles at a fair pace, resting but a little while upon the road, and was prepared to seize the first opportunity to act in a new direction. My heart was heavy with the sense of the foul play which had been practised; but my brain had become excited, and the spell of unrest was on me. I could not read or write—write even to my wife that night—I could not sleep for the hundred plans that rushed at me at once, and bewildered me by suggestions how to act. I was playing a game wherein every step was danger; my own life might be at stake if I aroused suspicion of my plans. I had need to adopt every precaution in my search; he whose policy was to baffle me was in the village again, watchful and vigilant.

The next day was Sunday; I was awake early, feverish for action. The day brought no sense of rest; my pulse was irregular, my incentive to be

up and stirring was a something irresistible. I,
who had thought so little of Ellen whilst my wife's
life trembled in the balance, who had let days and
weeks pass, half believing in the reports that had
been circulated against her, now begrudged every
minute filtering by, wherein my purpose rusted
from disuse.

I went for my old walk by the lower bank at the
water's side, to sketch out my next course calmly,
if it were possible. I chose the path that led
towards the wall of rock which closed the Vale in,
instead of proceeding down it past the Ferry.

It was seven in the morning, and there was no
one stirring. The honest Cumberland folk—the
few there were at Nettlewood—took a longer spell
of rest on Sunday, to make up for early rising in
the week. I went on slowly, passing the spot
where I had knelt and dragged Letty from the
water, in the early days when she was desperate
with jealousy; I left on my right the mansion of
Miss Ray, and stopped only at the low oaken fence
that kept intruders from that portion of Vaughan's
private grounds which was separated by the road-
way from the house itself, and extended to the water's edge. I wound my way up to the road-way,
passed between the two oaken fences, and then de-

scended on the other side to the lake again. I
noticed for the first time, with any degree of attention, a gate in the oaken fence that I passed; when
I was by the water's edge, and proceeding still
further on my wanderings, I wondered if Ellen
had stolen from her house that night, crossed the
road, passed through that gate to the lower grounds,
and then taken one leap from desolation to death.
The thought chilled me—but I experienced a
morbid satisfaction in brooding upon it, in specu-
lating upon its probabilities. It seemed possible,
even reconcilable with her strange demeanour on
that night I saw her last. Then my thoughts deepened; and it seemed also awfully reconcilable
with all that I had heard of Vaughan, that he
might have killed her in his passion, in his dash
for the freedom that would make him Letty's husband, and have stolen out in the dark night to
sink her body in the lake. I sat down on the bank
and pictured it—the solemn stillness of the night,
the darkness brooding over the mountain scenery,
the security from all witnesses save those who
looked from heaven—the figure, with its burden
creeping stealthily along the house, across the road,
through the gate, and down the winding path—the

one plash in the deep water that ended all, and hid all till the Judgment.

I sprang up, and shook away the thought at last—it was a cruel one, it was *not* reconcilable! The plain truth seemed to me, that Ellen had left her home, not to join Wenford, but to fly from danger. Some one had crossed the Ferry that night—cut the rope of the ferry-boat—and steered across the lake—why not Ellen?

Then once again came perplexity, to make my brain dizzy with these many speculations. In the lower grounds attached to Nettlewood House was a small private boat, seldom used, but handy for anyone of the establishment who might wish to cross the lake. Why should Ellen come down to the Ferry, if she wished to gain the opposite side, when means more handy were at her disposal? Was it not more likely that Ellen adopted this course, and that her husband, missing her at a later hour, came down to the Ferry Inn, and crossed the water in pursuit of her, by the only method available to him? In pursuit of her—by which route? By the Black Gap Pass, whence the pistol-shot sounded. Who fired that pistol, and what was the result?

A picture still more grim and horrible presented

itself. My heated imagination sketched the terri-
fied woman struggling on to Engerdale by the
mountain pass, and the destroyer following her. I
heard the pistol-shot, and the mountains murmur of horror at the deed; I saw the woman
falling forwards on her face, and the pursuer
hurrying on towards her in the spectral greyness
of that night. It was a horrible but natural conclusion. My next step must be to take the Black Gap
Pass, and carefully, vigilantly work my way, and
search for any sign that, by God's goodness, might
be left me there.

This became almost a settled conclusion with me
by which to regulate all future progress. The
more I brooded on the picture, the more reasonable-
ness there seemed to be in it. What step more
natural than that Ellen, fearing for her life, should
attempt to escape, and by the Black Gap Pass,
which she had once owned to me was a familiar
road to her?—where she spent her lonely hours in
musing on the hard fate that had befallen her, or
in sketching the wild landscapes that were ranged
round her from every point of view. In my port-
folio at home was one scene from the Black Gap,
drawn by her hand when the mists she feared had
not wholly closed around her.

I went homewards, fixed to one idea, that Ellen had attempted the Black Gap route to Borrowdale that night—the route that led to her mother's arms, where comfort and love were to be found —and that Herbert Vaughan had followed her. Between Vaughan and Wenford some desperate scheme had been concocted, which Ellen's forethought or flight had disturbed, perhaps, and hence the chase that followed. And yet my heart sank more and more. It was a leaden weight within me ; the more the impression of my new theory began to steep in upon my brain, the more heavily and laboriously my heart beat on.

If it were correct, the end was sad indeed. Vaughan had succeeded in his project, returned home by his own boat, left by Ellen on the other side of the stream, and appeared at the inn in the morning with his dastardly explanation of the mysteries of that night. I went on like a man walking in his sleep ; I took no heed of passing things ; I scarcely knew the route I followed ; it was instinct that brought me to the Ferry Inn.

What a struggle it was to descend to every-day-matters !—to talk to Jabez of the fine morning, to sympathize with him on the few English tourists who thought Nettlewood deserving of the honour of a visit, to eat my breakfast and prepare for my walk to Henlock Church, as though there were no gigantic evil shadowing my life, and no sister to find, living or dead!

Still I prepared for Henlock Church, with a purpose inapplicable to prayer; I could not pray; I could but think of Ellen, even in God's house, and take my schemes of vengeance with me there. Had it not been for seeking a still further clue, I should have attempted the Black Gap Pass that morning, but I suddenly remembered that Janet visited Henlock Church twice ever Sunday, and that she had once spoken strangely to me of Ellen's disappearance. She had never offered her own version of the little she might have heard or seen after Ellen's return from Mrs. Ray's, and she was a truthful woman, whom it was not difficult to trust. I felt that if her love for her master would stand as a shield between him and discovery, at least there was no fear that she would betray me to him.

I went to Henlock at an early hour, but met her not by the way. On the road an open carriage, containing Miss Ray the heiress, whirled by me, with Herbert Vaughan cantering by its side, looking as amiable and happy as though he had lost no wife, or known no shame. Miss Ray did not see me, she was listening attentively to all that her attendant had to say, and it was only Vaughan who bestowed upon me the faintest bend of the head by way of salutation.

It was a mockery of worship with me in the church that morning—the words of the reverend pastor floated unheeded by, were empty echoes reverberating amongst the rafters of the roof. I sat like a dullard, looking straight before me, at times so forgetful of church forms as to remain sitting whilst the congregation stood, and then leaping up suddenly and startling my neighbours. When Janet arrived, full half an hour late, my attention was directed towards her—she became the sole object of my careful watch.

Whether she were more abstracted that day, also, or whether it were her usual manner, which I had not thought of noticing before, certain it was that her demeanour at church was not much more reverent than my own. She sat in the free seats, that were ranged in the middle aisle, from the doors to the clerk's desk, taller by a head and shoulders than the young and old woman between whom she had taken her place. A remarkable object at any time—at that time, to me, one of unusual interest.

It was a hard, bony face, to which my attention
was directed—a face full of stern thoughts, which
gave it character, and even rendered it repellent.
She was thinking little of the prayers that were
being read to her—much that disturbed her heart
was expressed in the stony look before her. To
me she looked older and more worn—I fancied
that her hair was greyer, and not arranged with
that degree of tidiness for which she had ever been
remarkable. Hers had been a long watching of
my wife, and had tasked her, perhaps, beyond her
strength. Once the pew-opener whispered to her
as she passed, but Janet did not heed her until her
arm was touched, then she started and took the
hymn-book which had been proffered her, with a
scowl that might have annihilated the old woman
for her uncalled-for attention.

All that morning I watched Janet Mackersie.
During the sermon I observed that she looked
more than once towards Herbert Vaughan, sitting
by Miss Ray's side, an acknowledged suitor, ere
he was free to talk of love. That propinquity to
Letty Ray was my one distraction of the morning
—he sat there an insult to me, a slur upon the
fair fame of her he had traduced. But the indig-
nation faded away, and the one thought came

back, that the end was afar off and in darkness, and I had scarcely made one step towards it. The sermon was over, and they were streaming out of church at last, three-fourths of the congregation turning towards Henlock, the remainder proceeding back to Nettlewood. I went out with the rest in the same dream-like fashion, saw the carriage of Miss Ray rattle away, and Herbert Vaughan take the horse from his groom—a new groom—and ride after it, and then looked round for Janet, whom I detected striding homewards along the Nettlewood Road.

I set forth after Janet; I was a fast walker, but I found considerable difficulty in overtaking her. She strode on like a life-guardsman, swinging her long arms by her side at every step, and making rapid progress. I ran a little way at last, and came up with her by those means.

"Good morning, Janet."

She gave a little jump at my propinquity, and said,

"Measter Gear—ye started me."

"Did you not expect me at Henlock Church to-day ?"

"I thocht ye mayhap had gane back to Borrow-dale after the lassie. She be too narvous, too deli-

cate to leave alane there—she be too fond of worry
as to where ye'll be, and what ye'll be doing."

"I shall be going back next week—after all, it
is only a day's walk across the mountains."

"Ay!—that's true."

"Before I go, will you be a friend to me,
Janet? I have come to Henlock to-day to ask
that question."

The woman looked steadily at me. I could see
the face take a shade degree more hardness, as
though she suspected treason against her master's
house at once.

"I am a freend of a' who luve my Mary," she
said, however; "to ye, Measter Gear, I hope alwa'
to be ane, wi'oot bein' a traitor to my ain
sel."

"Now my wife is well, I am anxious about my
sister Ellen—I can know no happiness, Janet,
until the mystery of her disappearance is explained.
Will you help me?"

"How can I help ye?—how can I explain a
meestery sic as that?"

"Do you remember the night on which you and
I talked together in the Ferry Inn about my
sister? Oh! Janet, you opened your heart to me
somewhat that night."

"I war dazed— I war a fule!" she answered, doggedly.

"You told me that you were learning to love my sister when she went away—that she had a reason for her flight."

"Deed I?" she answered, cautiously.

"Will you tell me that reason?—will you tell me why she fled so suddenly and mysteriously away?"

"Measter Gear, ye ken naethin', and ye theenk too muckle of a' the nansense my head's been gallied wi'. I ken but leetle of the dark nicht's wark—it war beyon' a' guessin' o' mine, sir. If I war larnin to luve the lassie—she held aff and would na' trust me. She went awa' untrustin' me."

"Janet, she *did* go?"

Janet's colour changed—her eyeballs protruded—she glared at me with horror.

"Mon, do ye think her hoosband murdered her? Do ye think—do ye think," she said, in a husky whisper, "so bad o' him as that?"

"I have no faith in him, and only fear for any living thing that stands in his way."

"Ye are awfu' hard, sir," said Janet, resuming her stolid demeanour; "had I anythin' to sae, I

could na' tak ye into my confedence after a' that
ye ha'e spak to me.   Sir, I stand by him still, and
luve him still," she cried with true dignity; "do
ye ask me to be a spy upo' him?"

"I ask you, Janet, by the love you bear my
wife, by my wife's love for you, and by her anxiety
and love for Ellen, to tell me in what manner my
sister left her husband's home?"

"I canna tell."

"Janet!" I cried.

"I ken ony that she did leave.   If it wull make
ye happier, I can tak my oath she left the hoose."

"Janet, I will take your word.   You have been
ever a faithful friend—you saved my wife's life—
I have no need to think myself deceived."

"May I ask ye a question?" she said, curiously.

"Yes."

"What new schame be this, that ha gi'en ye so
wild a luke, and made ye theenk of puir Mrs.
Vaughan just now?"

"He is thinking of marrying again—of casting
her aside who took his name, and of holding her up
to a shame which I feel is undeserved."

"Ye canna sae—it's a' awfu' dark!"

"I must defend her, Janet—I must discover
Ellen."

"Wull—ye are her brither—ye luve her, and ha' a richt to defend her. But I think ye wull waste yer time—I see nae gude, and muckle harm, to follow sic a step."

"Janet, you will not help me?" I said, reproachfully.

"I tell ye, I hae na power. And I tell ye, if I had," turning upon me with a fierce face, "I wud na muve my leetle finger. Ha' I luved the bairn sae lang, to turn agin him at sae late an hoor?"

"In God's cause—why not?"

"Ye shall na tell me that I've lost a' hope o' him—I hold firm still—I dinna giv' wa'—my heart's na mair breaking than yer ain!"

She brandished the hand that held her prayer-book in the air, and then as suddenly calmed, and assumed her grim inflexibility of visage.

"Ye wull na truble me mair," she entreated; "I'm e'er yer freend, for Mary's sake—I wish ye, wi' my auld heart, a' happiness thegither."

"Thank you, Janet."

"Gin ye gang back to Borrowdale next week, I may na meet ye again—I may ne'er see ye again, Tak' my luve to Mary—dinna harass her aboot a past that was nae verra happy—God bless ye baith !"

She strode out at a pace more rapid, as if she closed the conversation by those means. I made no effort to overtake her; I saw how futile further attempts would be to learn more of Ellen—even if more concerning her were known by Janet.

I let her go her way ahead of me—stern, dogged, and faithful. I felt that Ellen had left Nettle-wood House on the twenty-first of July last. In which direction, it became now my task to ascertain.

CHAPTER III.

ANOTHER DEFENDER.

THE incidents of that Sunday were not over yet. Whilst I was at my early dinner in the best parlour of the Ferry Inn, a message was brought that Miss Ray would be glad to see me in the course of the afternoon.

It was close on four o'clock when I presented myself at Miss Ray's house, obedient to the request of its proprietress. The servant ushered me into the handsomely furnished drawing-room where Mrs. Ray had received her guests a few weeks since—where the daughter sat awaiting me. As I entered by one door I observed that the governess, under whom Letty was still finishing her long-delayed education, departed by the other.

"Good afternoon, Mr. Gear," said she, rising for a moment, "this is a strange day to choose for business, you will think."

"It depends whether it be urgent, Miss Ray."

"It is urgent only so far as it concerns myself," she replied. "Pray, be seated, and favour me by your attention."

"Willingly."

I sat down at some little distance from the handsome girl—growing more handsome and graceful, it seemed, as she became more educated. Looking at her then, so lady-like and stately—the fitting mistress of so fine a house—the old Ferry days went further and further back, and were scarcely reconcilable with that time.

"Mr. Gear, I am going to London for a few weeks—possibly for a few months. I have grown very tired of Nettlewood."

"Change is good for all of us, Miss Ray."

"I said once that I objected to the name of Miss Ray from those friends belonging to the past estate," she said, with a slight exhibition of irritation. "But no matter—possibly it is preferable between us now."

"I trust that I have not lost *caste* in your estimation latterly?"

"No—have I?"

This was asked with something of her old
brusqueness, and I smiled as I replied,

"Why should I think less of you—hold you in
less estimation than in the old days, Miss Ray?"

"I may tell you presently—we are speaking
of business, in the first place."

"The business that takes you to London?"

"Business does not take me to London," she answered quickly; "on the contrary, I wish to leave
behind here all business in your hands. You are
a friend in whom I can trust, Mr. Gear—one of
the few friends I possess still."

I bowed my head to the compliment. I had no
reply to make just then; I waited for further ex-
planations. She made them, fluttering a cost-
ly fan in her hand the while, in a fine lady-
fashion which she had learned of her governess,
mayhap, but which irritated me a little with its
seeming affectation.

"I leave for London very early in the morning
—I am anxious to arrange with you a few details
before I go. These alterations—how long will
they take now?"

"A fortnight more perhaps. As far as my own supervision is concerned, I think I can afford to turn to other business away from here at once. Like yourself, I am very tired of Nettlewood."

"The associations connected therewith are not pleasant, Mr. Gear," she said, her white brow contracting a little, "but I would beg you to endure them for a while. I wish you to remain here in this house as my steward—what you will—and keep watch and ward over the estate. I have been thinking of building a school-house in the neighbourhood, and shall be glad to see your plans and estimate."

"Thank you, Miss Ray," I answered, "but you must allow me to decline the stewardship—you must even let me postpone all further business in Nettlewood for a while. I am very anxious to be gone."

"The house can take care of itself then," she said a little abruptly; "it was suggested to me, and I fancied that the offer might have appeared suitable to you. You might have found time to look round the village, and choose your own site for the school I mention. I am very anxious to build that school—to do some little good here."

"I do not decline this offer, Miss Ray—consi-

dering that it concerns my partner's interest as
well as my own, I have no right to do so. But
for a while, and so far as regards myself, I *must*
be free."

"You are unsettled," she said, regarding me
steadfastly.

"Very," I confessed.

"You are troubled concerning your sister still?"

"Pardon me," I interrupted quickly, "that is a
forbidden subject, and I am sure you will not intentionally pain me."

"Oh! I will not speak of her again," she said,
fluttering her fan more violently, "it is an un-
pleasant subject, as well as a forbidden one. I am
glad to see that your wounded pride turns from all
mention of her name."

"My wounded pride!"

"She was ever unworthy of you, sir. Strange
that in brother and sister there should be at times
so wide a difference."

"Ay—an awful difference," I muttered.

I was thinking of Vaughan and my wife at that
moment, and Miss Ray's first remark—woman's
stern and hasty verdict on one of her own sex—
passed me unheeded by.

"Then I may not hope that you will remain here during my absence, Mr. Gear?"

"I am compelled to leave."

"Your wife is at Borrowdale—you will be glad to return to her?"

"Yes."

"I cannot blame you—I can sometimes," with a smile, "envy you a little."

It was a smile that told of her own content in the present, her own hope in the future—not the forced smile that had seemed once akin to pain.

"You are going to London, you tell me, Miss Ray," I said, rising, "it is scarcely a city in which a young girl, alone like yourself, can feel at home."

"My companion attends me—Mr. Vaughan will be in London to protect me."

The name was brought intentionally into the dialogue—I marked the effort, the flush that stole over her face, the steady gaze she directed towards me whilst she spoke.

"I am sorry for that," I exclaimed.

The words escaped me—overleaped the guard I had set upon my tongue. I was anxious to de-cline all business in Nettlewood, and take my departure coldly, avoiding all discussion of topics that might be dangerous to treat upon. But I had thrown down the gauntlet, and it was snatched up on the instant. I believe she had been waiting for an opportunity to defend Herbert Vaughan.

" Why sorry ?"

The ice once broken, I spoke out.

" I am sorry, Miss Ray, because the days are early yet to acknowledge Mr. Vaughan your suitor —because Mr. Vaughan has still to prove his poor wife's infidelity."

" It will be proved, sir—if there were a doubt about it, would I allow him to see me for an instant?"

" It would have been more maidenly to wait."

I had thought this long since, and I did not spare her the avowal.

" I scarcely comprehend yet what is considered maidenly in polite society," she said ; " where the heart is concerned, I follow its dictates, and care little for those who consider themselves justified to harshly criticize. I love him, sir,—and I am proud to own it."

" Great heaven! why do you love that man ?"

" Great heaven! sir," she exclaimed, passionately, " why have you so long misjudged him—

why, in your selfish interest for her who has disgraced him, do you feel no pity, no respect for one who thinks and speaks always highly of yourself?"

"I am flattered by his opinion of me—I regret that it is impossible to return it. I regret still more to hear you love him——"

"I have loved him all my life," she interrupted; "you, who have known all that that life has been, can guess how I have struggled with my passion, borne with it, let it sweep me almost to death, in despair of it ever becoming something higher, better than it was. I loved him when he was beneath me—I loved him when his wife was turning against him, and there was no sympathy between them—it is the proudest triumph of my life to think he seeks that love at last, and looks to it in the future as the one comfort I can bring him for his life-long injury."

She struck the fan upon the table as she spoke, and shivered it to atoms. She sprung to her feet and stood erect, with flashing eyes and heaving bosom. Her passion robbed me of my stoicism; her wilful blindness to the object with which he sought her out; her wilful abnegation of all that had once lowered him in her eyes, by demonstrating his true character, led me to speak more sternly in return.

"I will not have it injury," I cried, as warmly as herself; "no injury wrought by my sister's hand has fallen upon him. God knows the reasons that led my sister's steps away from home and husband—I will not question them, I ask for them forbearance. More, Letty Ray, I warn you—I feel that I must warn you—of one who destroyed my sister's happiness, and he will have no mercy upon yours."

"I—I cannot listen to this, Mr. Gear—I will not listen!" she cried.

"I warn you as the friend you styled me but a moment since—the friend who wishes you all happiness, and prophesied that it would come to you one day. I ask you to pause—to reflect—to remember every action in the past wherein your faith was less in Herbert Vaughan."

"All that drove me nearly mad in the past has been explained, sir," she said, proudly; "do not taunt me with my own ignorance and folly. It is not your place—it is unbecoming a gentleman."

"Miss Ray, I will say no more."

I bowed, and moved towards the door. When

I held the door open in my hand she called me—
even came towards me.

"Mr. Gear," with a faint smile, "we will part
friends, at least. You are the victim of a strange
hallucination, and I will not let it rob me of my
esteem for much that is good and noble in your
character. To Mr. Vaughan, whom it might pain,
I will say nothing of the particulars of our interview—I will wait the time wherein you will think
more generously of him and me."

"Miss Ray, I do not distrust *you.*"

"You distrust my *maidenly* reserve—in my conduct you see much to blame."

"In your place, even with your love, I should
certainly have paused awhile, Miss Ray, but I do
not distrust you."

"Before his wife deserted him, he made me the
confidante of the doubts that were preying upon
him, and I strove to re-assure him by speaking,
even against my own conviction, in your sister's
favour. When those doubts were verified, I could
not turn away and say it was 'unmaidenly' to give
him comfort in his trouble."

"Still——"

She interrupted me; she would hear no more.

"I tell you that I know nothing of the world—

that only a little while ago I was an ignorant
village girl," she cried; "I tell you here again
that, rich or poor, I will never set that world between me and a generous impulse, and I will
never care to study it!"

"If you would only promise me to study human
nature and its motives more closely for a while,"
I said.

It was reviving the old grievance, but I could
not forbear. Young, handsome, wealthy, I saw
her, blinded by her love, walking on to the abyss,
trusting in the hand which led her to the brink.
I saw her in the future, when Vaughan was free,
perhaps, following in my sister's track, adding one
more victim to the sacrifice. I saw the infatuation that possessed her; I knew the power of the
man to please, to disguise, to ensnare, and, under
any circumstances, I beheld a life that might have
gained its share of sunshine, sinking from the light
and all human effort powerless to save her.

"I will make that promise *with you*," she answered to my last appeal.

"I am already studying human nature."

"With a bandage over your eyes," was her quick,
almost laughing response.

I did not laugh with her; I bowed gravely over

the hand she held towards me, and prayed silently
for her awakening. In the fate that lay beyond
for her, there was nought to raise a smile in
me.

"All letters written to me here will be for-
warded on," she said. "If you will let me have
your account, I shall be glad to settle it."

"Thank you."

So ended this talk of "business." So parted
Letty Ray and I for many a long day.

CHAPTER IV.

AMONGST THE MOUNTAINS.

FOR what reason did Herbert Vaughan profess so much attachment to myself—speak ever of me as one whom he wished to call his friend.

That was the question which I asked myself, proceeding back towards the inn. Was it to contrast my own bitter enmity towards him; to deceive her further by his false airs of amiability even to his enemies?—or, by persistence, to hope in finally deceiving me?

But the curtain had dropped between the past and him; he would have stood aghast, and I should

have made an enemy of him at last, could he have
known all that his sister had divulged to me.
There was no mystery in his character after that
dread revelation—by all that he had acted in the
past, and she suspected, I could guess all that he
had dared to do. I could believe that Ellen had
met with foul play at his hands, and spurn indignantly away the crafty lie which accounted for
her disappearance.

Each hour that passed, more firmly strengthened
me in the belief that Ellen was dead—and that
not far from me were hidden the awful proofs.
Every hope of seeing her again, of holding her to
my heart once more, had withered, and there was
not one blossom of hope left. To find her in her
unhallowed resting-place, and bring her murderer
to bay was all my purpose now. I should not rest,
night or day, until I solved the mystery; every
turning of the tortuous road that baffled me but
strengthened my dogged resolution to search on.

I rose early the next morning, prepared to search
the Black Gap Pass, continue my route to Borrowdale, and see my wife and mother ere my restlessness drove me forth a wanderer once more.

Over my breakfast, which I could scarcely
touch, I studied the last present Ellen had given

me—the pencil drawings of the Ferry, and the mountains seen from the Black Gap range. The latter interested me most; it was the scene to which I was drawn, where my suspicions lay, whither Ellen had been fond of wandering. She knew every turn of the road, she confessed to me when giving me the sketch—surely she went this way then, as safer for herself, and wherein it was more likely to elude pursuit.

Drawn by her skilful hand it was a gloomy picture enough—from the range of mountains this side of Engerdale River, separating the two gaps, she had sketched very truthfully the desolateness of the landscape. I had caught a glimpse of it in the murky twilight, when the mists were driving, at me in the valley on the only time I tried the pass; here was a faithful transcript of the vale I had hurried through, and the mountain land that hemmed it in. The sheep-fold lay in a hollow close against the mountain side—a few hasty pencil-marks presented it to the eye, an utter ruin, in unison with the wildness of the scene. Ellen had put her initials to the drawing—E. V.—on a stone, or boulder, that was close against the sheep-fold—it looked so like a tomb, belettered thus, that I shuddered and laid down the sketch.

"I am growing superstitious," I muttered, rising to look at the sky, and read therefrom an augury of the weather. A sky clouded and unsettled as myself—giving no promise of rain, perhaps, as the day was clear and the mountain tops stood out rugged and sharp,—but a cold disheartening heaven, with leadeny clouds floating slowly along, a screen between the sunshine and the earth which yearned for it.

I was ready to depart. Ellen's sketches were in the breast-pocket of my coat; I had slung a knapsack on my back; to the foreman of the works, who had visited me that morning, I had left all requisite instructions; days, weeks, or months might elapse before I stood again in Nettlewood—all was uncertainty, all pursuits in life were flat, unprofitable, and devoid of interest—the face of my wife was but the one bright spot in the dead vista of the Beyond.

Jabez, himself ferried me across the lake, and reddened and stammered when I offered to shake hands with him.

"Thankee, sir," he said, "it's koind o' ye. We're all sorry you're going—we're hoping you'll soon be back again."

"In good time, perhaps."

"Nettlewood's got to be—that is, it ain't got to be—like Nettlewood a bit without you. I'm sure that you'll come back, sir."

When I turned towards the field across which lay the route to the Black Gap, he said,

"You mean to try the gaps atween the Fells, sir?"

"Yes—shall I have fine weather?"

"I think the rain'll keep off a soight o' toim. You're roight eno' to-day, and if you loike clambring, why it's the best way hoome."

"I fancy so myself. Good day."

"Good day to you, sir—good day. Allus good luck to you, Mr. Gear!"

And with this benediction from the honest countryman, I turned my back on Nettlewood once more.

The day was before me; I was not pressed for time; I wished to proceed on my journey slowly and critically, following, in imagination, Ellen's footsteps, and trying to fancy whither they would have led her in the darkness. I do not know why I should have regarded this journey through the Gaps as an important proceeding on my part; what motive impelled me to expect the faintest sign of incidents which had happened a month

since. It was a fallacy to expect a sign, and yet I
went on looking for it, as though Ellen had left
Nettlewood but yesterday, or the route had been
forbidden ground since July last. Half-a-dozen
miners, quarrymen, and shepherds trod it almost
every day; tourists, straying from the tourist's
beaten track in the Lake district, occasionally
imitated their example; what was there left for
me to base one hope or fear upon?

Still I went on, trusting to find some fragment
of a dress, torn, soiled, and trodden under foot,
that might betoken Ellen had been here, or to note
some evidence of a deadly struggle, which had left
the ground disturbed still. I studied intently the
ground apart from the beaten track, rather than
the regular line of pathway up the mountain;
pursuer and pursued might have strayed
out of course, and casual passers-by were not
likely to be particularly observant. Half-way up
the steep ascent the circuitous path turned sharply
to the right, following on led slowly upwards
again, and ended in a jutting point of ironstone,
from which was a fall of a thousand feet or more.
I deviated from the path, and wound my way to
the crag, finding nothing by the way. On the
crag I sat down to rest awhile, and looked down

on Nettlewood, so still and peaceful a resting-place in the green bosom of the valley.

Could it be possible, thought I, that in that quiet spot of English country, where but half a dozen houses represented the village, so much mystery and crime had sprung; that from a place where peace seemed eternally to rest, had evolved such evil, and seethed such awful passions? Looking down upon it, it was a fair scene enough—a welcome contrast to the mountains shutting it in, and frowning down upon it in their rugged majesty. The valley and lakes were strips of green and silver, which I thought might be closed in at any moment by a forward movement of the hills on either side, and shut away for ever. Landslips had happened in these parts before, I had read in the dog's-eared guide-book at the Ferry Inn—it did not appear so impossible an event to blot Nettlewood eternally out of English topography.

In the little spot below me what a deal had happened to influence my life, and the lives of those I loved! Leaving the Great City, wherein every street had its romance, and every house its mystery—where tragedies were acted every day, and men, whose lives were matter for a thousand

books, brushed you in the crowded streets, I left
all peace of mind behind me, and in this silent
place plunged into the turmoil! Strange accident, or strange working of destiny by Him who
acknowledges no accident, Below, there I had
made my first step in life, met my first love, been
drawn to her by her struggles and her fears, won
her for my wife through all the plotting that went
on against us both, saw acted there, and played a
part myself in, a drama of wild plot and underplot,
on which the curtain had suddenly dropped
and left all interested wondering what the end was!

"Would the end ever be arrived at?" I thought
as I retraced my steps to the regular footpath, up
the Black Gap; "or ten years, twenty years hence
should I and Mary still be left to wonder at it all?
—to tell our children what strange things had
happened in our day and néver come to light?"

The rain kept off, although no break of
sunshine occurred during my progress; no wind
was stirring, all was very quiet round me.
Amongst the mountains there reigned a stillness
singularly impressing—one felt hidden away from
the world there. A bend of the track—if track
it could be called any longer—shut Nettlewood away from me; I was far on my way now;

I was ascending, then descending where the land dipped; then reascending, at times a little puzzled as to the direct route. If Ellen had come this way that night, missed her way, and gone wandering on in the darkness, how easy to fall into one of these hollows, and be heard of no more, or be found, months afterwards, by a horrified shepherd, whose dog had strayed away to rouse the echoes of the hills with its discovery. Such things had happened—might happen again.

Engerdale! On the high land I looked down upon it. I had passed through the gap, there were heavy-browed rocks piled on all sides of me. My steps led downward to a valley more silent than Nettlewood, possessing not one single inhabited house for miles, disturbed alone by the murmur of the river that wound its solitary course down the vale, and was fed by the leaping, hurrying "Force," which broke its way from the rock, and dashed tumultuously towards it—a valley shut in more closely and in more sombre fashion than Nettlewood by dark verdureless hills. Engerdale Vale they called this in the guide-books—"'Tween the Gaps" was its more homely and more fitting designation.

I looked at my watch—the hour was only eleven
in the morning; there were yet many hours of
daylight before me.   If I searched this vale mi-
nutely, some little evidence of all that might have
happened therein would surely reward my search.
There had been few observant eyes this way;
travellers hurried through it and across the river,
only anxious to press forward; more than one
Cumberland superstition was connected with this
place, and no native cared to wander hither save
in the bright sunshine.

When Ellen gave me her pencil sketches, she
told me of this vale—what a favourite spot it
was, from its very loneliness, from the strange
effect produced in the midst of its sombreness by
the hoarse murmur of the "Force," and the rip-
pling of the restless water against the stones in the
river-bed.

I drew forth her sketch, and compared it with
the landscape—almost from my own point of view
had the drawing been taken—here meandered,
faint and circuitous, the stony path downwards;
there was the valley and the stepping-stones across
the stream; and the ruin of the sheep-fold against
the rocks.   I went down slowly to the vale, with
the sketch in my hand, as though it were a map

which Ellen had left me of her wanderings; I stood amongst the rank grass of the vale, where a few sheep, lank and bony, had strolled from some remote district; I crossed the stream, now less swollen by rains than when I first waded through it in the early days; I broke from the track, and wandered through a mass of wild herbage and jagged bits of rock that had glided from the mountain side, towards the fold which some farmer, long gathered to his fathers, had knocked together as a refuge for his sheep when the storm met them 'tween the gaps.

"Hard pressed by one who sought her life, this would have struck her as a fair hiding-place," I muttered, when I stood surveying the ruin which a hundred storms had left there.

CHAPTER V.

THE SHEEP-FOLD.

IT was a larger building than I had expected to
discover; dwarfed by perspective, it had seemed a
little wooden shed rent by wind and rain, and
cowering in the shadow of the rock.   Close upon
it, I found it a long low edifice, constructed of
rough-hewn timber, and standing about ten paces
from the mountain, in lieu of resting against it, as in
the picture she had drawn.   It was an utter ruin.
Built round the angle of the rock, the wind had
yet found power enough to burst its sides in, strip
half the red tiles from the roof, render it an un-
comfortable resting-place even for the sheep.
The side nearest the river had been boarded in,

whilst the other side had been left open, its con-
structor having laboured under the delusion that
the rock at some little distance was sufficient protection from the storm for quadrupeds. The roof
was supported from within by a few cross beams
and pillars, formed of hewn branches of a tree
that had been lopped down in the neighbourhood,
and fixed there in all their native ruggedness.

The cross beams were open to the sky now,
and fragments of the red tile that had formed
the roof were scattered about the ground beneath. Only at one extremity had the wind
been charitable, and left a square yard of
tiling, over which some lichens had grown luxu-
riantly, and were peeping down into the silent
shadowy fold. The planks, weather-beaten and
storm-driven, were dashed in in many places, one
rough piece of timber supporting the roof had
been snapped in twain and the lower parts left
jagged and splintered. Entering the sheep-fold
from the back, I stood and looked at the wreck of
good intentions represented by this ruin. The
place was full of shadow, and had an unearthly
aspect beneath the leaden sky that lowered through
the rent roof; the grass was growing beneath my
feet; the fragments of rocks had found their way

there; one heavy boulder had evidently been hurled
from the mountains in some hurricane, and gone
crashing through the roof into the fold; the lichens
were growing within, and decay and dry-rot were
slowly but surely levelling the frail tenement to
earth.

The fold possessed one occupant—a stolid sheep
curled in the darkest corner of the place, too
feeble and sick to hurry away at my approach.
It lay panting in the corner, and blinking at me
as I stood there; wherever I turned, its eyes looked
after me distrustfully.

I raked amongst the grass and stones with the
point of the walking-stick I had brought with me,
but no sign of the past came to the surface. Here
had ended all hope of finding Ellen. I must follow
on the old track and discover Wenford, and endeavour to learn from him the share that he had had in
the mystery, and why he left on the very night that
Ellen went away. My nervous fancies had, after
all, deceived me—Ellen had not come this way, or
hidden hereabouts. I sat down on the ground at
last, with my back against the wood-work of the
fold, and tried to think of the best course to
follow after this, and whether it were not wise of
me to retrace my steps and pursue my route along

the car-road which skirted the Black Gap range
of mountains. Yet I was strangely disposed to
linger here—my nervous fancies had not all dis-
persed, and I could believe that in this ruin I was
more near the truth—more near Ellen's grave!
In such a place as this, had she been pursued, she
would have hidden; in such a place, had she been
murdered, would her body have been buried.

I tried to assume the part of a murderer myself,
and to imagine what I should do in a spot like
this burdened with the dead form of my victim.
I could not leave it in the vale; the river was too
shallow to sink it in; in this ruin it seemed only
possible to bury it. I stood up again, and tried
the earth with my heel; I poked at the sick sheep
to induce it to move; finally, I put my arms round
it and dragged it to the opposite corner, it bleating
plaintively meanwhile. Where the sheep had
lain, something crushed and soiled riveted my attention—one slight proof for which I had been
searching through the day. I made one dash towards it, clutched it in my hand, and glared at it
with suspended breath.

" He was here that night—I swear it!" I ejaculated.

It was a glove that I had found—a yellow kid

glove, stitched in an eccentric manner with black.
He wore gloves of that kind on the night I saw
him at Mrs. Ray's—the very night of Ellen's
flight. I remembered on the instant that my
attention had been directed to them then—I was
sure that this was one of them!

I was on the track—God had mercifully afforded me one sign of all the evil that had been
practised here. From this what might not follow?
—there was the whole vale to search now—every
turn and hollow of the mountains, till they opened
into the village some ten miles lower down. I
would search every spot, and know no rest till I
had discovered further trace—I swore it there
upon my knees, with my heart plunging and my
temples throbbing wildly. I placed the glove
carefully in my pocket-book, and then tried the
earth on which the glove had lain, but it was hard
and rock-like, and gave forth a ringing sound that
told of its remaining undisturbed since the sheep-
fold was built over it. I sat down to ponder on
the new course that lay open to me; a sickening
sense of nausea was upon me—if there *had* been a
faint hope of Ellen before then, it had vanished
with that discovery. I felt assured that Herbert
Vaughan would not have coolly asserted the

gigantic lie he had framed to hide her guilt, if she were living to refute it. It was a lie that turned suspicion at once from him, and did not spare her in her grave.

Though the sky was open to me, and the little air that was stirring came soughing through the rents and fissures, the place felt stifling and unhealthy. I made a movement to depart at last, and rose with that intention, when a footfall on the stones without arrested me. A footfall that came on at a rapid pace, and turned the corner of the fold where it was open to all comers—a footfall that stopped suddenly.

I looked up; Herbert Vaughan stood looking in upon me, a man rooted to the spot by horror at the sight of me. I saw his face change—the ashen greyness replace the healthful look it always bore —even for an instant the lower jaw drop with a vacuousness of expression that wholly changed the naturally keen countenance.

" Gear !" he gasped.

I was surprised by his appearance there; for a moment he took me off my guard, and I clutched my stick more firmly in my hands, as though I feared an attempt upon my own life.

"What has brought you to this place?" he asked.

My first impression was that I had been watched, but when I noted his unnatural paleness, his complete bewilderment at thus suddenly coming upon me in this place, I felt that it was a chance meeting, and that he had been led hither to search—possibly not for the first time—for the glove that lay about here, one witness which might rise against him, and defeat the scheme he had in view.

I was on my guard then, and answered:

"I am returning home to Borrowdale, Mr. Vaughan."

"You have chosen a strange resting-place," he said.

"Surely no stranger for you than me, sir."

He had gained his self-command—he was an admirable actor.

"I saw you from the higher land, and came hither after you. I am going to Borrowdale also—thence to London. I could not let the opportunity slip to offer you my hand again—for the last time to tell you that your unnatural want of friendliness towards me pains me, and that by any effort, by any sacrifice, I would live it down."

" Mr. Vaughan, we are best apart," I said, passing from the fold into the vale; " I do not believe in your friendship—I would rather that you told me frankly how much you hated me, and feared my power to work you harm."

" To work me harm," he said, keeping step with me, and regarding me with eyes that glittered somewhat, " I fear no man's power to do that. Why should I fear yours, my sister's husband, more than others?—why should you, of all men, wish to do me evil?"

" I am a man in search of a sad truth," I answered; " if, finding that, I tread you under foot, I cannot help it."

Neither could I help my excitement in that moment—my warning that there was much that I suspected, and was seeking a solution for. If I were led by this to show my purpose too plainly, to put him on his guard, and set his wily brain to still more securely baffle me, it was beyond my power to disguise the abhorrence that I felt for him.

" If your sad truth means the discovery of your sister's shame, follow it to the end. You may respect me more when you are face to face with it— when you have found her, and she owns her guilt to you. But to tread me under foot, Canute Gear, is beyond your malice, and your threats are idle to me."

"I threaten not."

He looked at me with a strange irresolution. In his heart, I knew that I was a mystery to him. For the first time in his life, perhaps, he feared my grave persistence; found that his own specious phrases, his own apparent frankness of demeanour, only warned me of the nature he attempted to conceal thereby. He could not judge me accurately; my movements were undecipherable to him; my presence at the very place to which he had been drawn, had startled him with a sense of danger from which he had believed himself exempt.

"Mr. Gear," he said, after a long pause, "I can only attribute this iron reserve to one cause. It is a hard one—it is an unjust one. My sister, in a weak moment, has spoken against me, and you have listened to her morbid fancies, and believed in them. If I be right in my surmise, I claim the right to answer any doubts of yours."

"I require no answer, sir—I make no accusation."

"For the last time," he cried, with some excitement on his own part, "I offer you the hand of a friend. For the last time I tell you that I would be your friend, ask your advice, give you a brother's place in my heart, work with you, even to find Ellen. For the last time, Gear, will you sink the bygones, and let me teach you to respect me more?"

He held his hand forth; knowing him to be a villain, I yet was staggered by his manner for an instant. Then the stern truth came back and steeled me.

"I am not your friend."

"You are my enemy then—I am to be ever prepared against you. I see you working in the dark, and following some foolish theory which you have framed concerning me. You are my enemy, and must take the consequences."

His suave manner vanished, and the hand that I had rejected he clenched, and shook towards me. On his face then I saw the real expression of his heart, and felt how deadly and desperate was his nature.

He went on before me towards the White Gap, strode up the steep ascent, and turned not to look back till he was many hundred feet above me,

where the first height was attained and the hill
dipped. Then, with the grey sky backing his
dark figure, he turned and looked down at me
standing where he had left me last, with the river
at my feet. He shook his clenched hand at me
again and disappeared.

* * * * *

I reached Borrowdale four hours later. No
further incident had met me by the way, no further
proof of the one crime which shadowed everything,
had come to light. I had toiled on slowly; I had
gone back more than once; I had taken twenty
different paths away from the direct route, and,
with difficulty, retraced my steps—I arrived home
very worn and weary, but strengthened more than
ever to follow in my search, and to study the
Vale of Engerdale next day.

HOME! What a relief it was, after all the
intense anxiety of the day!—notwithstanding that
I crossed the threshold with my one load of doubt
still heavy on my mind.

They were not expecting me, my mother and
Mary. This was a surprise for them, which I had
built on somewhat, and I was rewarded by their

cry of delight, and their joyful running forward to meet me.

Mary had heard the click of the wicket-gate, and was in my arms before my mother, not so agile as herself, had made her way to the open porch. In the evening sunset, my wife and I went up the garden-path together.

"I am so glad, Canute—I was growing tired of home without you, and pining to get back to Nettlewood."

"To get back to Nettlewood—how strangely that sounds!"

"Anywhere—where you are!" she said, adding, with more eagerness, "oh, Canute! you must never leave me for long! Whatever takes you away, must not take you without me. I fear for you more than myself, when we are separated."

"Well, we will not talk of parting, Mary, in the first moments of this meeting. Has he been here—your brother?"

"No."

She looked up, with a scared white face, at once dreading danger on the instant.

"He passed through Borrowdale this afternoon

—probably he rode from Keswick to Bowness, as he seemed anxious to reach London."

" He did not come here."

My mother met us at this juncture, and clasped her fond arms round me.

" My dear boy, this is more like home now. Mary and I have been trying to think this home without you, and make the best we could out of your absence. But—oh, dear !—what a difference you make ! "

" Thank you," I said, " I am glad to see that you appreciate the advantages of my presence."

The light vein I had assumed did not elicit a smile from her, however ; there were thoughts too grave and deep for much smiling in those dim latter days. On her face I saw the lines of care more deeply graven, or, in my own selfish pursuits, I had not remarked them much when she was helping to nurse Mary. Still my forced air of cheerfulness deceived her, for she said at once,

" Have you heard from Ellen ? "

" No,"

" Not a line ? Never a word to the old mother, who prays that she may think of her, and write to her, and tell her that she repents even at the last."

"Hush!—hush!" I said. "We will not judge her, mother. God alone knows the motives which took her from her home, and you and I, at least, should be the last to think them guilty ones."

"Don't you think—oh! don't you think her guilty?"

"I do not."

"Oh, Canute!—I thought not until I came home here—and then I got foolish and superstitious about the willow—you will not laugh at me for that?"

"About the willow—what do you mean?"

"Come with me—you don't know how it has troubled me."

We turned back down the garden path, and went along the country-road a little way, towards my mother's cottage, then closed and untenanted whilst she kept Mary company. We did not enter the house, but passed round by the broad side-garden to the back where the willow, planted in its youth by Ellen's hand had been set when my mother brought it from London. It had given promise of flourishing there when I had seen it last—now it was withered and dead.

"It shrivelled up suddenly—I left it green and strong, Canute."

"The lightning perhaps—or something at the root. We must not believe in auguries—or see cause for grief in a willow-tree dying, mother."

"I knew you would scold me," she said, wiping her eyes; "but I was always a little superstitious, and it came on me quite a shock, dear. It has always been a part of Ellen to me, something ·by which I always remembered her and loved her. I grew to love the tree for her sake—almost to fancy that whilst it grew and flourished, she would flourish too. I can almost fancy—don't scold me again, my son—that her life died out with the willow's."

My wife caught my arm, and looked up at me. She and I had long since given up all hope of Ellen's life—only the mother clung to that hope still, and knew nothing of our secret.

"Would you rather hear that she had died, mother, or that she had fled to infamy?"

"Heaven help me!" exclaimed my mother. "I would rather hear that she was living still, waiting God's good time to repent, and come back to my arms."

It was a mother's wish, and I said no more concerning it. She clung to her one hope, and I had not the heart to dash it down. I could not tell her of my own belief—or point to the stricken tree, and say,

"So suddenly and unaccountably passed Ellen from life unto death!"

END OF BOOK VI.

BOOK VII.

PLOTTING.

" Who charges guilt on me?

" *Mustapha.*—Who charges guilt !
  Ask of thy heart; attend the voice of conscience—
  Who charges guilt ! Lay by this proud resentment
  That fires thy cheek and elevates thy mien,
  Nor thus usurp the dignity of virtue."
JOHNSON.

" Why, there's an end then."
EDWARD MOORE.

CHAPTER I.

FELLOW-SEARCHERS.

I LINGERED not many days at Borrowdale. I had no heart to sit still and take comfort from the home affections; till the darkness round Ellen's last days was rolled away like a cloud, I felt a guilty coward idling time there. In a few months were to come, with God's will, a great happiness, and a new source of joy—I had feared their being dashed away from me in the sad hours of Mary's illness, but the hopes were living still.

My course was difficult to follow out under these circumstances, for Mary became more restless and excitable; the fear of danger befalling me in some unexpected form, rendered her anxious con-

cerning my safety, and my own confidence did not
reassure her.   Though the past was no longer hidden from me, and I knew all that she had feared
and suffered therein, yet she still entertained the
one nervous objection to dilate upon it.   For my
sake she had told me all her fears, all her trials in
the early days before we knew each other; she
had offered me the clue to the dark labyrinth of
her brother's life, but she did not care to follow it.
That grim past did not stand now between her and
me, and she was content; drop the veil over it
again, and save her from the phantoms which kept
her mind disturbed with the fear of their approach.
To speak of the past to her was to make her
colour change, and hold her breath suspended; to
speak of Ellen was to bring back all the fears that
she had had for her—more than all, the weakness
and agitation from which she had heretofore
suffered.

Hers was not a bold spirit made to combat stern
truths; hers was a nature that required support,
the love and protection of one who could think for
her, and be her shield against her own supersti-
tions.   She was a woman to love with her whole
heart, and to be loved—but she was a fragile
flower, and unfriendly elements had overtasked

her strength. I could not seek counsel of her, confess to her all my bitter thoughts and vain imaginings—could not tell her the whole truth.

It was a strange, almost a sad position, against which I had no right to complain—against which I never thought of complaining. Her very weakness had helped to strengthen my love for her before my marriage; her child-like confidence in me kept my love pure and bright in those days wherein one stern idea possessed me, and I knew no consolation for it.

I did not look forward to the end; to the time when the secret might be wrested from Herbert Vaughan, and I require just expiation for it. What might happen when the end was reached, I did not care to dwell upon. The ascent was steep · and the distance far—I was content to go on slowly, surely; taking no heed of the time when crime should be brought to bay, and I should have to act sternly and decisively. When that time came, sufficient opportunity for me to resolve to shield or to avenge—I could not sketch that meeting face to face yet, or say, "Thus will I strike him down," when the hour came to place him at my mercy.

Concerning him, I was compelled to speak

when I mentioned my determination to proceed again to Nettlewood, and work backwards from the inn at Triesdale, to which place I had tracked Mad Wenford. I had lost all trace of Ellen; through Wenford it might. be possible to gather at least one hint or two concerning her or Vaughan, which might set me once more on the track.

"You will not be long away, dearest?" my wife said.

"But a few days—possibly a week."

"If you are longer away, you will write to me and let me join you? I am very unhappy in your absence—I have great fears for you."

"Mary, I cannot rest. I must find Ellen, or some trace of her."

"Yes," she sighed, "it is but natural. But in searching for the sister, you will not forget the wife?"

"Do you think I shall?" I asked her.

She was in my arms at that appeal; her dear impulsiveness brought her to that shelter where she felt most confidence.

"No, no!" she cried. "I have no fear of that. I am only weak and superstitious, and cannot explain all the follies that bewilder me. Sometimes," dropping her voice to a whisper, "when I am grieving for your absence and pining for a sight of this dear honest face again, I feel haunted by a spirit—*hers!*"

"Why, this is childish indeed, my dear girl."

"Haunted by her and her reproaches," continued Mary, in the same excited manner, "hearing a far-off whisper as though she chided me for that selfishness which would keep you at my side, or screen him who has been so strange a brother to me."

"You must not think of this," I said, firmly; "better to accompany me, and share all my doubts and fears than this. If I am likely to be long away, I shall write for you to join me."

She looked relieved, and my mother entering gave a turn to the conversation. That very evening, when Mary had preceded me to our room by a few moments, I told my mother of all that I had resolved upon.

"I believe I have a clue to the discovery of Mr. Wenford," I said. "I think it necessary to seek him out, if possible."

"It may be necessary—God knows, my dear—I don't," answered my mother.

"I shall see Mr. Sanderson in the morning, and throw myself upon his generosity again. I fear I am but a poor partner for him, at this juncture."

"Why don't you write to Joseph?" asked my mother.

"To Joseph!"

In the whirl of events that had engulphed me, I had almost forgotten him. His life lay so far apart from mine, ran on in so different a groove, and was actuated by motives so foreign to my own, that he had scarcely cost me a minute's speculation since I had parted from him last.

"He is out of business, and has but little to do," added my mother; "I am sure, for my sake and yours, he would make every necessary inquiry in London, and save you much trouble and expense. He had always so shrewd a head, my dear, if you remember."

Poor mother! I had not shaken her confidence in her eldest-born's honesty and shrewdness—I had let him keep, perhaps, the first place in her heart, and hidden the story, which he had confessed, of his own baseness, far away from her whose motherly love had reared an idol from such crude materials. She had ever admired that tact —to give it no harsher term—which had made Joseph a rich man; which had placed him at the head of the family, and I let him keep his place there, and even sang his praises to keep one honest soul from breaking down. Latterly she had known much tribulation—was not the mother of the old days, who could gather her children round her in a few hours—let her life pass as smoothly on to the end as God would allow, and I could make it!

I professed to have forgotten Joseph's shrewdness—even promised to call upon him, compare notes, and profit by his wisdom, if the chance presented itself. My mother knew his address; he had written to her once at Borrowdale, to ask if anything had been learned of Ellen; and for that symptom of interest in one who had been his favourite, I forgave Joseph all past trespasses. He had been a cold, hard man, whom nothing seemed to affect, and I read his letters with a new feeling of charity towards him. There was no shadow of the narrow-mindedness which had characterized his life upon the hastily-scrawled sheet. I had forgotten, almost, that Ellen was his sister as well as mine, until that night.

"If you know anything of Ellen," he wrote, "if you or Canute have heard of anything, however trivial it may seem, concerning her, I hope you will write to me at once."

My mother had written some weeks back, telling
him of her inability to offer one scrap of intelli-
gence concerning her daughter, of my wife's illness, and my own prostration, and nothing had
been heard of Joseph Gear since that time. I took
his address down in my pocket-book, and then
followed my wife to her room.   The next day I
set forth once more for Nettlewood, having previously seen my partner, and confessed my inability to work whilst tossed on that sea of uncertainty, which had surged round my quiet home.

"I can spare you, my lad," was his generous
answer; "if there were any one whom I loved,
that was lost to me, or in danger, you would spare
me, I think, and not grumble at the double duty."

"I think not."

"Then God speed you, Gear."

So with this blessing on my enterprise, in which,
after all, he had but little confidence,—as I learned
in the future days when we were working together,
—I set forth anew upon my search.

I hurried through Nettlewood and Horley to
Quirkett's Farm and Triesdale; I threaded the
Triesdale Pass, and took up my quarters at the inn
where the clue had been obtained of Baines and
Wenford.   Thence, slowly and deliberately, I

worked my way onwards, baffled often, but defeated never, obtaining here and there a proof—vague and indefinite, but still a proof—of those two men, going on together, still in company, and still unattended by a third, who might have worked her way towards them from a quarter less likely to be watched.

With difficulty at last I traced them, or fancied that I had traced them, by railway to Liverpool. Here, by consulting files of newspapers, &c., I learned what ships had left the Mersey during that week, and whither they had been bound. Here the magnitude of my task began to appal me; here fifty speculations as to the future course of those two men began to bewilder me; here once more into the foreground came the doubts as to whether the result to be arrived at were worthy of the search, or whether it were not already sufficiently evident that Ellen Gear's disappearance had no connection with the departure of Wenford and Baines for Liverpool. Still I did not give up; by dint of much research I ascertained the names of the ships that had sailed for all quarters of the world on the day and following the day that Wenford and Baines arrived there.

A steamer for Canada from Wellington Dock;

a steamer for Gibraltar, Genoa, and Leghorn; a
steamer to Rotterdam from Nelson Dock; a steamer
to the West Coast of Africa from the North
Landing stage; a steamer to New York from Hus-
kisson Dock, had sailed within the week, together
with a host of smaller steamers for the seaport
towns of Ireland, Scotland, Wales, and England.

I directed my attention to the Rotterdam, the
Canadian, and the New York steam-packets in
particular; if I failed in any information to be
derived from the shipping agents, the task
became almost beyond me. Wenford and Baines
might have sailed to one of the seaport towns, or
even have gone from Liverpool to London—in the
swelling crowd of human life at this great mart of
the world's commerce, further clue to them verged
on the impossible.

I visited the shipping agents, calling at last
upon those for the New York line of packets. I
had been all day unsuccessful. Lists of the passengers who had sailed by those particular steamers
alluded to had been submitted to my inspection;
every information had been tendered me by the
courteous clerks to whom I had made known my
wishes, but the further I proceeded, the greater
became my difficulties.

I entered the office of the agents for the New York line of packets, tired and dispirited. I had had a hope that I should have found some trace of two passengers arriving late for the Rotterdam or Canadian steamers, and, failing therein, I had not much confidence in any further efforts. After all, I was but human, gifted with none of those rare faculties of penetration for which a few men, here and there, are celebrated—only following on where it was easy to follow, and baffled just as easily as my fellow-men. I had been over-confident, and not realized sufficiently the magnitude of that task which in the latter hours loomed before me, and now cast upon me the whole weight of its depressing influence.

The office was about to close when I arrived. A sallow-faced clerk, with his hat on, was consulting with another over an unwieldy ledger; both looked up as I entered, the sallow-faced man turning off one of the burners above his head, by way of a significant hint to me.

" Could I see the list of passengers who left for New York by your vessel, the Cormorant, on the 24th of July last?"

" You can to-morrow, sir—we can't attend to any more business to-night."

"What time to-morrow?"

"Oh! nine or ten—when you please, in fact," was the off-hand answer.

"Thank you."

I was leaving the office when the younger clerk, who had hitherto continued poring over the ledger, said suddenly—

"What date did you say?"

"The 24th of July, 18—," I repeated.

"That's the second inquiry to-day we have had about that ship, isn't it, Mapleson?"

Mapleson muttered a gruff negative, and the clerk answered sharply—

"Yes, it is."

"Well, then, it *is*," said the sallow-faced man, who was anxious to get home and keep down argument.

"What did you say it wasn't for, then," said the young clerk; "you're always saying it wasn't. Didn't you talk about the man being small enough to be put under a glass shade, and ugly enough to be exhibited as a curiosity?"

"Oh! did he want that list? Very likely—good night."

And out went the sallow-faced man, whose example, after a moment's hesitation, I followed. I

went my own way when in the narrow street,
resolving in my mind the glimpse of something
new and strange which the little sparring match
between the clerks had afforded me. I coupled
everything that happened now with my own particular case, and attributed at once the inquiry
for the list to some one interested, like myself, in
following these men. A man, whose small stature
and ill-looks had struck one of these clerks, at
least—whom did I know of spare figure and
countenance not the most winning in the world?
Joseph Gear !

I stood at the corner of the street to think of
this. Joseph Gear, my brother, who left Nettlewood on the morning following Ellen's flight—he
who had written to my mother, asking for news of
Ellen—he who shared with me the shame which
one man would cast at us in his effort to be free,
a man whom Joseph Gear confessed to hate, and
would take no small trouble to circumvent. Surely,
there was a chance of my brother being engaged
on the same errand, working with me, and beside
me in the hope of finding her.

CHAPTER II.

COMPARING NOTES.

REVOLVING this, and more than this, in my mind,
I returned to my hotel, more perplexed than ever.
If Joseph Gear were on the track also, how was
it possible to find him and compare notes?   I
thought of his parsimonious habits, of the saving
impulse which had led him at Nettlewood to take
refuge in the common room of the Ferry Inn,
rather than be burthened with the extra expense
of a private room, and fancied it might be possible
to discover him by his idiosyncrasy.   He was, to
a certain extent, a nervous man, therefore to a
very low inn he would not resort, for fear of being

robbed; he was, to a great extent, an economical man, therefore would have asked at the railway-station, or of a policeman, providing he had made no inquiry in London, as to the whereabouts of a decent and cheap inn. In the coffee-room was Bradshaw's Railway-Guide, which I took up in the hope of discovering a few advertisements of inns at Liverpool. In this I was not disappointed —and, selecting two from the number, who held forth the advantages of good recommendation and moderate terms, I set forth in search of them. I found the inns with little difficulty, but gathered thereat no tidings of Joseph Gear —no gentleman answering my brother's description was lodging, or had been lodging there; the names of all comers were hard to arrive at—I might step into the coffee-room and look round for myself.

Everything being done, and everything failing, I went on to the railway-station, intending to inquire of a chance official where was the cheapest inn to be found—to put myself in Joseph's position, and assume, for a while, so far as it was possible, his particular weakness. I felt assured that if he had arrived a stranger to Liverpool he would not have left the station without harassing all who

were able to afford him information by a hundred
questions as to board and lodging.

There was a bustle at the great station; the
government, or parliamentary train for London
was on the point of starting—those bound London-
wards were pushing and tumbling over each other
in their eagerness to secure the best positions, to
see to their luggage, to find comfortable corners
wherein they might curl themselves and be rattled
off to sleep in due course; the guards were extra
busy, and not inclined to pay much attention to
any inquiries foreign to the business on hand. I
sat down to wait till the train had departed, and
left the officials time to breathe; very unreal and
dream-like a position it appeared to be, sitting quietly there in a noisy railway-terminus, with the hurry
of a world beside me—unconcerned about a seat
near or far away from the engine, disturbed not by
thoughts of a long journey, and friends or enemies
waiting at the end thereof; caring little about the
train being behindhand, or of the express following it in half an hour; content to sit there
apart and moralize upon the travellers, and feel
that with the joys and sorrows, pleasures, pains, or
love of money that took them on their way, I
held not a single share.

I thought so, and was mistaken. For shuffling towards the train, at a rate peculiarly his own, with a tiny carpet-bag in one hand, and a walking-stick in the other, there suddenly passed me Joseph Gear. I sprang to my feet, ran after him, and laid my hand upon his shoulder.

"Joseph!" I exclaimed, "stay! I want you—I am seeking you!"

My brother turned round, dropped his carpet-bag, picked it up with a trembling hand, and stared hard at me, as at a phantom.

"Good gracious!—whoever would have thought of finding you here!" he exclaimed.

He was too much amazed to offer to shake hands with me; he stood and stared, till I motioned him to follow me apart from the bustle.

"But—but I'm going to London."

"You must go by the next train."

"I've paid for the ticket," said he, ruefully.

"I'll pay for the next, if they will not accept the difference," I said. "Stop with me for a while —you must!"

"Very well," he said, with a half-sigh over the

waste of money incurred by my precipitate act.
" Now, what's the matter ? "

" Sit down here, and I'll tell you."

Joseph sat down near me, and put his carpet-
bag and stick beside him. Once he glanced nervously into my face, as though fearful of the nature
of my avowal, This I noticed.

" What do you fear ?" I asked.

" I thought' that, perhaps, you had turned
against me—that the story I told you once had
rankled just a little, and made your feelings less
brotherly towards me."

" I think but very little of the story, Joseph,"
I replied. " I am doing my best to forget
it."

" Thank you," he said, humbly.

" If you will give it a moment's thought,
you may guess the errand that brings me
hither."

" I don't see how that is possible."

" What brought you to Liverpool ? "

" Business, Canute—a little private matter of
business—that's all."

Joseph's caution perplexed me — annoyed
me. What object could he have in this reserve.

"You came here on the same errand as myself. You were at the office of Messrs. Watson, Young, and Co., the shipping-agents for New York, this afternoon—you looked at the list of passengers, who left this port by the ship Cormorant, on the 24th of July."

Joseph continued to stare at me; his face to express every instant a greater degree of amazement.

"How did you find all this out?" he gasped.

"By chance. I am in search of our sister, stolen away or murdered, on the last night you spent in Nettlewood."

"Hush!—don't talk so loud as that! Are you mad?"

He looked round, and then dropped his voice to a whisper.

"We don't know whom we may put on guard," he said. "It is best to proceed slowly and cautiously."

"You are in search of Ellen?"

"Yes."

"You do not believe that she eloped with Mr. Wenford?"

"No."

I shook him by the hand again—I felt drawn towards him by ties that, imperceptibly, had weakened, or been broken years ago—he was my brother again, in whom I could trust.

"Let us compare notes—you and I working together may hit on some fresh clue."   .

"What have you found out?" he asked, with no small eagerness.

Briefly and rapidly I communicated the particulars of my long and unavailing search; of my visit to Quirkett's Farm; the discovery of the horses; the tracking of the two fugitives to Triesdale Inn; of my breaking off that clue to follow the one which led me across the Black Gap; of the discovery of the glove in the sheep-fold; of my interview with Vaughan there; of all further trace vanishing away, and leaving nothing to guess at; of my renewed search after Wenford, ending with my meeting Joseph Gear.

He had listened very attentively to my communication, only once distracted in the beginning of my recital by the departure of the railway-train. At that juncture he sighed again, and said,

"There it goes—sixteen and ninepence—oh, Lord!"

When it had rattled away out of the terminus, he crossed his hands on his knees, and attended to the rest of my story. At its conclusion, he drew a long breath, and said,

"Ah! there's not much in it, after all!"

"What have you discovered?"

I saw the extra shade of caution stealing over his face—the resolve to keep back some portion of his own story. In the first hesitative stammer, I checked him somewhat indignantly.

"Tell me all, or nothing. If you do not see that our motive is alike, our interests alike, in this sad case—if you fear to put your trust in me, in fact—why, keep your secret to yourself."

"I have every confidence in you, Canute," he said; "don't fire up so. You have grown so impetuous that it is difficult to understand you. I—I even think that we might work together, comparing notes at certain intervals, and following each his plan of action, till we run him to his death."

He clenched one thin hand, and beat it on his knee. I knew of whom he spoke, without mention of a name between us. I saw that love for Ellen was not so much the ruling agent, as hate for him whom Ellen had loved and married.

"That man has ruined me," he said; "and if the time comes for my turn I will not spare him. Canute," he added, "I have not discovered more than yourself—that is, not much more—and I am only going to London now to work in my own silent way a little plan of mine, which may lead to something—which may not. I'll tell you of that plan when we meet again—say, when I write to you, which I will presently—but there is nothing now I care to inform you about *that*."

"Very well," I responded coldly.

"It's only my own bait to catch a fish," he said, with a little feeble laugh of self-conceit; "I was always sharp enough, you know."

"Sharp enough," I said, as a grim remembrance shot through my brain like a pang, "oh! yes—that's true."

"What I have done, I have no objection to tell you, Canute," he said in a conciliatory tone; "you have not told me anything of your future. That's all guess-work, and worth nothing perhaps."

This was true also.

"Well—what have you done for Ellen's sake?"

"I have, by very hard work, tracked Wenford and a man of the name of Baines—such a damned scoundrel, Canute!—to this place. Losing scent in one direction, I tried this, like yourself."

"Successfully?"

"Yes—-I think so. They left for New York on the 24th of July last."

"You are sure of that?"

"Yes—entering their names with much bravado as Edmund Wenford, of Nettlewood, and James Baines, servant to the above. They arrived in Liverpool only two hours before the vessel sailed, and had some difficulty in obtaining a passage, the vessel having its complement of passengers."

"They went away together. In that list there was no name of——"

"Ellen Vaughan—yes, there was."

"Good God!"

"Take it quietly, Canute. It should not deceive you. It did not me. That was a stroke of cunning on the part of them, but I think I see the reason for it all. That's a flimsy piece of duplicity, that should not deceive a sharp race like the Gears."

"What do you think?"

"That some woman was bribed by those men to personate Ellen Gear—to pay for her passage to New York by that name. If Herbert Vaughan wishes for a divorce, he must pave his ground carefully, you see. Women ready for any mischief are no more hard to find in Liverpool than London."

"We must discover the captain of the Cormorant."

"I have found him. I saw him but half an hour ago. He does not remember much about the passengers, save that there was amongst them a very tall man calling himself Wenford, and a lady—a brazen-faced lady, he said—who called herself Mrs. Vaughan. I have no proof that is decisive yet, but I can swear that that woman was not Ellen."

"I must go to New York," I cried.

"That would be folly," said my brother; "that would be falling into the trap they have set for us, and getting one of us at least comfortably out of the way. Ellen never left England—Ellen was dead when that vessel sailed across the Atlantic."

"You think so too!"

"Yes."

"Now tell me why you think so," I said; "you were awake and restless on that night of mystery; you did not sleep that night, but wandered about the banks of the lake—whom did you see cross the Ferry?"

Joseph looked on the flagstones, then at me.

" No one," he said at last.

" Is this true?"

" I went on towards Henlock; when I returned, the ferry-boat was gone. I heard the pistol shot at twenty-five minutes past two, and timed it by my watch. I scented danger, and waited for it till the grey morning, when I entered the Inn and fell asleep, worn out with watching. But Canute, in crossing by the Black Gap later that day, in following on the steps of those who fled from murder, and those who thought of it, I found this ring."

He rummaged in his waistcoat pocket, and finally produced a little circlet of emeralds and pearls.

" It's a small ring, but it cost me, wholesale price, three pounds ten and sixpence," he said; " I gave it her upon her birth-day once."

" Yes—and—"

" And I will swear it was upon our sister's finger the night we saw her at Mrs. Ray's party."

I held my breath suspended. What if all that was presaged by that evidence had been guessed at and prepared for?—what if I had become con-

vinced that Ellen was no longer of the living?—
still the shock fell with no lighter weight upon my
throbbing heart.

"We have not to study that man Wenford
much—or care much· for this divorce case, that
may be followed up or not," he said; "we have to
search for Ellen's body, and bring her murderer
to justice. That murderer is in London, where I
am going to watch him—your task is to return to
Nettlewood, and search the Gaps night and day for
further trace of her. She is hidden in the mountains, Canute!"

"It is my fear. It has been always my fear."

"There is not much evidence against him yet—
Vaughan might intimate that Ellen had fled by the
Black Gap, and joined Wenford at Liverpool. As
for the glove, that is a hard matter to bring home
to him, and if brought home would not stand for
much. Where is this sheep-fold?—how did I
manage to miss it?"

I told him.

"Search that sheep-fold again, Canute," he hissed;
"we shall have him yet. You're a sharper man
than I ever gave you credit for—poor Ellen was
sharp, too; how did she manage to fall into this
trap so easily?"

"You have not one faint hope that she may have eluded him?"

"Would she remain silent all this while?—is she a woman to sit still and have her name and honour stolen from her?"

"No," I answered.

"Then I think we'll see about this ticket, and if we can get it exchanged for an express one by paying the difference," said Joseph, "I'll tell them I was too late for the train."

"Tell them that you were detained—that's the truth."

"So's the other, or I shouldn't be sitting here," he said, with a slight titter, which verged on the idiotic.

He went away, and returned after a while with an express ticket in his hand. Sitting down by my side, he sat and fidgeted with it, dropped it on the pavement, picked it up again, keeping it ever before my sight in a demonstrative manner. I took the hint at last, and inquired what the difference was between his parliamentary ticket and the express. He told me, adding:

"I should be sorry to take the money, if I were not so poorly off now. When I have the upper hand of Herbert Vaughan, I may get all the

money back he swindled me out of. When he
marries——"

"He shall never marry Miss Ray," I exclaimed;
"do you build on that, and our sister's shame at
once, then?"

"No, Canute," he replied; "I am only building on finding out his secret. But if he did
marry her, all the greater disgrace for them both
when the truth comes out. *She's* no friend of
mine," he added, between his set teeth; "I haven't
forgotten my lady's interference. And I should
be very sorry to take the money, Canute, but it
was your own offer, and I can't afford to travel by
express."

"There's the money," I said.

"And I expect that's the train getting ready,"
he said, rising, after thanking me for my donation.
"I must not lose that, or my chance of getting a
good seat. I'm very tired—I'm very much worried
—I'm not half so strong as I used to be."

"You will write to me when there is any news
worth communicating?"

"Yes, I will—upon my honour."

He seemed anxious to dismiss the subject; he
had told me all, and did not care to discuss the
matter further. He was feverishly impatient to

be gone; anxious to be quit of me now there was no more to be learned from me, and, perhaps, something of his future plans to be betrayed, if I pressed him closely. He took refuge in the train, and curled himself in the extremest corner away from the platform—looking a little aggrieved when I followed him, and took my place opposite.

"You're not going to London?" he said.

"No. But I will see you off."

"Thank you," he said, closing his eyes; "how my head aches, to be sure."

He opened his eyes when a stout old gentleman, followed by a foreign-looking man, with rings in his ears, entered the carriage also.

"Good-bye, Canute," he said.

"Good-bye."

When he shook hands with me, I held him firmly in my grip, and looked steadily in those little twinkling eyes.

"Have you told me all?" I asked; "is there anything worth knowing, any clue worth following, which you keep back from me?"

"Why do you distrust me?" he asked, sulkily. "Why should I keep anything away from you?"

"God knows—I don't!"

"I give you my word that I will write when the

time comes," he said. "Good-bye. Remember me to mother."

I left the carriage; the bustle on the platform had begun again. Travellers of a higher caste than those who had thronged the place before, were getting into their places, and harassing the guards. When I quitted the train, and stood by the door, Joseph crossed over, and sat by the window to exchange a few more words with me. His last remark had reminded him of family ties, and he asked after his mother and my wife's health.

After a while, the train was ready to depart. The guard had slammed to all the doors; only a few were loitering like myself, and exchanging farewell greetings. The guard in charge ran the length of the train, and then whistled; the piercing note of the hissing engine shrieked out by way of response—the express train began to move.

Joseph's face beamed again with the joy of getting rid of me; by the light of the station-lamps I read that fact pretty plainly.

"Good-bye," I reiterated.

"Good-bye, Canute," he said; "work with me down at Nettlewood—keep quiet, but confident. We shall run him to earth, be sure of that!"

He went away, confident and exulting. I did

not like the expression on that withered face which glided away from me into the dark night beyond the station-lights ; once again I felt divided from him by every wish and thought that should have bound us together—us two children of a widowed mother !

CHAPTER III.

THE CITATIONS.

TIME went on, and brought no further clue.
Days, weeks, and months sped on with me and
mine; from spring to summer, from summer to
the ripe autumn time, and no news of Ellen, no
signs of Ellen's resting-place.

I had returned to Borrowdale and Nettlewood.
I had striven hard for my partner's sake to sober
down to work, escaping in my fitful moods to the
Gaps once or twice a week, and searching con-
tinually and diligently for any further trace of the
tragedy that had had existence there.

No further discovery, save the finding of a
miner's tool shed, if discovery that could be called;

the time stealing on, and the summer leaves fluttering from the trees. The mystery still deep and
impenetrable, only that secret ever before me to
mar the happiness which had come to me and mine
in the quiet home at Borrowdale. A child had
been born to us, and my wife was well and strong
again. All had gone peacefully with our little
circle; the fairy-face of the first-born lit up home,
and rendered it something still more pure and holy.
We christened it Ellen, after her who was lost to
us for ever; and my mother cried over it, and
prayed that it might be the blessing that Ellen in
her younger days had been to her. Of my love,
or of the passionate adoration of my wife for that
child, I need not dwell on here; proud young
mothers and fathers have experienced all that I
refrain from alluding to in this place, all that is too
subtle and deep for any writing to attempt.

Early in November, then, we were well, and
happiness not too far distant from us; my
wife was stronger, brighter, looked less fearlessly
at the future than I had ever known her.

"One more to love me, and to trust in me,
Canute," she said, hugging the babe in her arms;
"further and further away all the old shadows of
the life that has gone."

I did not know then that nearer and nearer to us was coming the shame we deserved not, and the dishonour we could not fend off.

In the interim between the present time and my interview with Joseph, I had not been idle in my inquiries; I had made them in all directions, and taken many notes which might seem apart from the one purpose which directed me, and yet which might afford a clue to hidden motives some day. Failing in all search for Ellen, I set myself to study the downfall of Edmund Wenford, to learn how a long course of recklessness, even profligacy, had brought him finally to ruin. To a certain extent I learned his history; he had been born in the great house that had "come to the hammer," and was well known in the Vale. Scarcely a villager in the place but had a story to tell of him and his eccentricities. I noted that the oldest folk —those who remembered him longest—spoke the most charitably of him; in the early days there were reminiscences connected with him less harsh and repulsive; one could almost trace how he went step by step downwards, knowing no moral counsellor, meeting not with one true friend.

Father and mother had both died young, and left him alone in the world, and the heir to a large property—lo! the old, old story, when the guiding reins are severed, the wilful is free to act, and the tempter is at the elbow.

"This man was not wholly bad," I thought; "if I could but find him, and throw myself upon his generosity to tell me all he knows of Ellen."

I wrote to Joseph once or twice, only to my last letter receiving an answer to the earnest question, "Was there any news?"

"No news of any importance," was his answer; "but I am watching them. Should they come to Nettlewood, watch them in your turn."

But they stayed away. The servants at Nettlewood House, and at the mansion I had planned for my wife, and which she had given up to Mrs. Ray, were on board-wages; only the new-comer and family at Wenford's house gave life to the quiet village. It was a dull time, and bad for the little trade that had existence there. I visited Nettlewood but seldom; there was little to take me across the Ferry after the alterations at Mrs. Ray's were complete, save the impulse to be stirring, and the hope of learning or of finding something more that appertained to Ellen's fate. Once or twice I crossed Janet in my wanderings, but made no further appeal to her. Strong in that strange love

K 2

for her master, there was little to glean from her
reticence.   Once or twice also Janet crossed the
Gaps, and made her appearance at our cottage.

"I ha' coom to see the wee lassie," she would
say, "and to make sure that ye are wull and happy,
Mary Gear."

Satisfied upon this last point, and maintaining
that she was well and happy herself, though her
face had become very old and care-worn, she would
take her departure once more across the Gaps—
doing the double journey in the day, as only Janet
could, perhaps, and resisting all inducements to prolong her stay.

In our quiet home we should have been akin to
happiness, had it not been for the thoughts of
one so wholly lost to us.   That grim truth stepped
between us and the light; checked the laugh at
times, threw over the house of rejoicing the shadow
of an unutterable fear.

The shadow deepened in the early days of
November—fell suddenly athwart us, and roused me
at least once more to action.   Mr. Sanderson had
sent me in yesterday's *Times* to read, and I was carefully studying it by the firelight that grey afternoon, whilst Mary sat opposite with her sleeping
baby, comfortably cradled in the chimney-corner.

My mother was at her own little cottage again ; welcome as she always was to us, she was a mother-in-law more wise in her generation that most mothers-in-law I have ever known or read of.

" My old-fashioned ways will not do for young folk like you—old-fashioned people never did live happily with those to whom the world is something fresher and brighter. Let me keep you in sight, and feel that I am as near to your home as your hearts, my children."

We were alone together then, sitting "between the lights" as the phrase runs. We had shared the newspaper between us in a fair and liberal manner, I coming in for the first sheet—the advertisement sheet—of the *Times*. To that portion of the paper I always turned in the first instance ; in that second column, full of mysterious calls and entreaties, I had a wild, visionary hope that something appertaining to my own case might appear. That something might be beyond all guessing at— it might be addressed to me, or a secret signal from Vaughan to those who were conspiring with him, or a message even from the dead to the living, telling of wrongs still unatoned for !

In that second column, on that November afternoon, there started into life that which affected

me. In this shape I had not prepared for it, and
I held the paper at arm's length, and groaned
aloud. My wife, ever on the alert, leaped to my
side at once.

"Canute, dear—what is it?"

"News—only news that affects us indirectly.
An advertisement in which well-known names
appear, and look somewhat strange in print."

I pointed to the advertisement, and read it
again with her by the firelight. It ran as follows :—

"IN HER MAJESTY'S COURT for DIVORCE and
MATRIMONIAL CAUSES.—To EDMUND WENFORD,
of 'The Larches,' Nettlewood, in the parish of
Henlock, in the county of Cumberland, gentleman.—Take notice, that a citation bearing date
the 14th day of August, 18—, has issued under
the seal of Her Majesty's Court for Divorce and
Matrimonial Causes, at the instance of Herbert
Arthur Vaughan, of Nettlewood House, in the
county of Cumberland, aforesaid, citing you to
appear in the said court within eight days from the
service thereof on you, inclusive of the day of
such service, then and there to answer the petition
of the said Herbert Arthur Vaughan, praying for

· a dissolution of his marriage with Ellen Vaughan ; and such citation contains an intimation that in default of your so doing, the said Court will proceed to hear the said petition proved in due course of law, and to pronounce sentence therein, your absence notwithstanding.—Dated this 13th of November, 18—."

Here followed the signature and the address of one Walter Effet, solicitor for petitioner, Chancery Lane.

Beneath this advertisement followed a second, addressed to Ellen Vaughan, giving the same notice of issue of citation to her—appearing to me the same mockery of justice, the same part and parcel of the craftiness which progressed so surely and safely to its end.

My wife had turned very pale ; in the fitful firelight I could see how white and anxious-looking she had become. Once again the past stole in and took its place with us there, the unbidden skeleton there was no shutting from us.

" What is to be done ?" she murmured.

" I must go to London—to this solicitor—to my brother. I must attend this trial and hear all that they dare to say of Ellen, and give the lie to them."

"You will not be rash—you will do nothing hastily, Canute."

"I must go away from here at once," I said, rising, "the place is stifling—shame and disgrace is coming to us—they are going to slander the dead!"

"Oh, my God! don't say that, Canute—I have been trying lately to believe that it may all turn out so differently."

"And in your heart what did you believe?"

She wrung her hands together, looked imploringly towards me and replied not. I answered for her.

"It was the worst! You who know best your brother's character, mistrust him most. There is no hoping against all that we know—there remains only one last effort to thwart Herbert Vaughan. I could not save her life—let me make one attempt at least to preserve her own good name."

"You will go to London?"

"Yes—at once."

"I must go with you—to take care of you," she added, with a faint smile, "I could not rest here with you away. We are hastening to the end, I am assured, Canute."

"Come with me, then—when the end comes,

and I am baffled perhaps, I shall want your presence by my side to comfort me."

"Courage, my Canute—you were never a man
to give way."

"No, no—I am strong yet. I will keep
strong !"

We began our journey that very evening—my
mother accompanying us also. She was anxious
too concerning all that would be said of Ellen at
the trial, all the evil speaking and slandering that
would be sworn to, and to which she could never
reply.

"I shall be handy as nurse to the baby also,"
she pleaded. " Oh ! Canute, you will not tell me
to remain here. Your trouble is mine, my son."

" Come then."

The desire to be stirring kept my blood at fever
heat. To be acting for Ellen in some way or
other ; to rouse my brother Joseph to make one
last effort to stay or postpone this trial ; to be stirring in the world, and striving to dash in to the
truth through the net-work spun round it—only to
be at work again for my dead sister's sake.

I think both wife and mother trembled for
me at that time—the phrensy so suddenly attacked
me. I reproached myself for resting idly when

there was so much to do; forgetting all that I had
attempted, and all that I had endeavoured to discover. From that moment when the well-known
names had started from the newspaper columns to
warn me of the time so near at hand, I knew no
moment's rest; I became irritable and variable; I
muttered to myself, and mourned over the little
time left me to act. I could think or talk of nothing else save Ellen and her husband; I forgot
my past consideration for my wife, that husband's
sister, and talked of the day of reparation—of the
day when, face to face with the awful truth, I
should confront him and set my foot upon him in
his base humiliation—of the vengeance, God and
man's, upon that awful crime.

My wife shrunk not away from me, but clung
to me the more, and would scarcely lose me from
her sight. She could not take her brother's
part—she could not say one word in his defence—
only once I heard her murmur in her sleep—

"I have done all this, it is my fault!"

I was becoming so wild and excited, that she
warned me of my mother's watchfulness, and of
all that my demeanour might betray to her. This
calmed me outwardly; for a while I had almost
forgotten my past promise to let my mother believe

that Ellen lived still—to let her believe in the lie which Vaughan had forged, rather than in the truth that would wholly break her heart.

When we had reached London, and had found quiet apartments in the New Road, my wife, ever solicitous, stole out of the house and brought in a medical man to see me.

" I could not rest," she whispered, as she introduced him into the room, which I was pacing like a maniac, "I am unhappy about you. Pray forgive me."

I must have verged upon mental derangement at that period, my actions were so strange. When the doctor told me I must keep quiet, and not give way to excitement, I laughed heartily, as at a pleasant jest; when he informed me that there was something on my mind, and I should make an effort to shake it off, or seek change of scene and employment, I laughed again; when his medicine came, I took up the bottle to shatter it against the bars of the fire-grate, when Mary suddenly arrested my hand.

"Do think more calmly, even of this, Canute," she urged; " surely, if you are hasty and precipitate, you will mar all."

" True."

I took the medicine as prescribed, and fell asleep shortly afterwards, conscious of the watchful eyes of my wife upon me all the while. I was more composed when I awoke; in the morning, though the same restlessness possessed me, my brain was cooler, and I was more prepared to act after my old fashion. To act in what manner, and in what direction?

After an early breakfast, I was thinking of setting forth in search of my brother, when he was announced.

"I have sent for him," said my wife; "I knew that you were anxious to see him, and that his coming hither would give you an hour or two's more rest."

"Ever considerate," I murmured; "but there is no time to rest."

When my brother entered, and after the first greetings were exchanged, my wife and mother left us together. The door had scarcely closed upon them, when I began at once to upbraid him.

"You have not treated me well, Joseph," I said; "you have kept all information back—this trial might have taken place, and the decree of a divorce obtained, and I never the wiser."

"Upon my honour, I should have written to you to-day."

"The hearing of this case—of all these fabrications, which have been hatched together by that man and his accomplices—how can we stop it?"

"It is hard to say what is best," said my brother. "You are so anxious to prevent the hearing of the case, you see."

"Why not?" I asked, sharply.

"If the case be heard, he binds himself to a statement which, in a little while, we shall be able to prove a lie. It will go all the more against him, when we face him with the truth. How he will writhe then, Canute!"

Joseph rubbed his thin hands together complacently. He was ever thinking of his own revenge—across his narrow mind the thoughts of Ellen's fame stole but seldom.

"Joseph Gear, I shall hate you presently!" I said, between my set teeth.

He looked at me in an alarmed manner, and edged his chair a little further away from me. He had been told last night of my excitement, and my wife's fears for me, and was on his guard.

"Keep cool, Canute, there's a good fellow," he remarked. "I've only a little while to stay, and cannot tell you all that I have heard, if you don't keep cool. There's business in the City, and——"

I leaped to my feet, ran to the door, and locked it. If I went beyond my usual self by that act, and verged again closely on the dangerous ground across which to sanity it is hard to return, my excitement stood me in good stead, and took Joseph wholly off his guard. He changed colour, and began to tremble.

"I will have no more of these half-confidences," I cried; "I will hear all, in return for all that I have told you. No plea of business must keep you from telling me your plans; what you, Ellen's brother, are going to do to save her name from being foully slandered in the courts of law. I will have no hanging back—I will know all that that there is to hope or fear—if you deceive me now at the last, I will have no mercy on you."

He thought I threatened him with the terrors of the law, for the act which had beggared my mother and me; and the threat had its effect, though I was not thinking of his past duplicity.

"I—I don't want to keep anything from you—

only be cool. The doctor says you're to be kept cool, Canute!"

"Go on."

"And you and I are brothers, one name, one flesh, with one hope in common. I'm sure you don't wish me any harm."

"Go on," I repeated.

"Well, then, I've found James Baines."

"The scoundrel!—where is he?"

"I knew that his relations were living here in London, and that if he ever came back from New York it was just possible he would come to see them. I knew that he would come forward as a witness, on Herbert Vaughan's side, being a man who would swear to anything, if he were handsomely paid for it. So I watched for him day after day, and set others to watch, and sure enough back he came, as I anticipated."

"You have spoken to him?"

"Not yet—I am not quite certain whether it is policy. But I have dogged his steps, and by that means I have found the hiding-place of conspirator Number Two."

"Edmund Wenford?"

"Yes."

"This is good news," I said; "the light breaks

in upon us—we must confront them at the Divorce
Court, in Ellen's name, or we must make one
great effort to stop the trial."

"I—I think we had better stop the trial,
perhaps," he said, "it's no good interfering. I
very much doubt if we have power to interfere, or
if any one would hear us."

"How can we stop it ?"

"By eliciting the truth from Wenford or
Baines, and then threatening Herbert Vaughan
with it, if he persist in carrying on the farce. By
making quite sure that Ellen never accompanied
Wenford to New York."

"Will Wenford or Baines confess that ?"

"I believe Wenford might be led to tell
the truth—I fancy he has been in part the tool of
others more wily than himself. If only some one
could be found to prey upon the little feelings he
possesses now—some one he had a respect for
once."

"My wife !" I ejaculated.

"Eh !—you don't mean that ?" asked Joseph,
eagerly.

"After his own fashion he loved my wife once
—I know that she had influence once to turn *him*
from evil thoughts respecting me."

"That's worth knowing—that's good hearing," said Joseph, decisively.

"Where is Wenford living?"

"He is hiding from his creditors in a street near Bermondsey. I will give you his address."

He drew forth his pocket-book, and scrawled a few lines in pencil on one of the blank pages, tearing out the page afterwards, and passing it to me.

"Your wife will be of valuable assistance to us, if she can move him from the purpose he has formed," he said.

"Have you seen him?"

"At a distance."

"How did you discover his hiding-place?"

"By dodging James Baines. He spends half his time passing from your brother-in-law's apartments to Wenford's."

"They are all in one plot, and have gone too far to retract," I groaned. "I see no hope to follow this."

"I am not so certain that Wenford is in the plot," said Joseph, nibbling at the corner of his pocket-book, and studying the carpet at his feet. "He's a wild drunken fellow, whom Vaughan would not trust more than he could help. My be-

lief is, that he was sent out of the way under
false pretences, and may even yet have but a vague
idea of the truth."

"He is as great a villain as the rest, I fear."

."Well, then, let the case be heard," said
Joseph, returning to his first scheme; "it may be
adjourned—I think we may get it adjourned for
further evidence, and then it will be easy to act.
I am going down to Nettlewood—I have another
clue to trace, I only require time."

"You are thinking of that money to which your
soul has been bound so long," I shouted at him
again; "in your foul cupidity, those who should
have been dear to you are not considered. Man,
you had feelings in your breast once; you loved
Ellen once; your heart *was* possible to touch. Be
honest, generous, think less of yourself; teach me,
by your better, nobler actions, to respect you
more."

"Keep cool—keep cool, Canute. Whatever did
you lock the door for?"

"We must see Wenford—failing Wenford,
we must see Vaughan, and warn him that we can
prove his accomplice sailed to New York, unaccompanied by our sister. I believe that man
will pause, when we tell him that Ellen and he

were in the Black Gap together on the 21st of July last year."

"We can't prove it.   If I could only bring that home to him."

"Ellen's ring—his glove."

"The glove is no evidence, for it can't be sworn to—the ring is.   Canute," dropping his voice to a whisper, "I should be more happy in my mind if I could bring that fact to bear upon the case ; if I could prove that Vaughan went to the Gaps after his departure from Mrs. Ray's. He gains the advantage of us for a while—*for he never left his house.*"

"How do you know that ?"

"I don't think he did—I don't believe he did— I was watching the Ferry all night."

"Joseph—you have not told me all yet."

"Not quite all—I'm coming to it by degrees, but you will not keep cool, and you don't encourage confidence."

"There—I am cool enough now."

"Patience then."

He drew his chair nearer to me, and laid one hand upon my knee.

"What I am going to tell you I did not communicate at Liverpool, because I had no faith in your powers of self-command; and a precipitate action might have put cautious people on their guard. Now, when we must both act very decisively, it is time to speak out, perhaps. Are you cool enough to listen, do you think?"

" Yes—yes."

" When Mrs. Ray declined the offer of my hand, notwithstanding the quantity of port-wine she had drunk, I went away too disappointed and vexed to care about any rest for that night. I had taken, perhaps, a little too much myself, and fancied that a walk would do me good by the banks of the lake. I told you once that I wandered on to Henlock—this was not true. I wandered to and fro before the Inn until I heard hasty footsteps coming along the high road in the dead of night."

I held my breath with suspense; nearer and nearer to the truth I felt advancing now.

" When I was certain that my imagination had not deceived me—keep cool, there's a good fellow! —I hid myself in the shadow of the house, and waited for the mystery to clear up. The footsteps approached, and came on towards the Ferry. I peered out, and saw plainly enough through the haziness of the night a woman at the water-side, striving with impatient fingers to loosen the cord that secured the ferry-boat to the landing-stage.

The cord was fastened in a way she did not understand, and with some sharp instrument I saw her cut it through, and, springing into the boat, seize an oar, and push herself away from land. Her face was turned towards me as she did so, and the moon broke out for a moment, and lit it up in all its ghastliness."

" And that face ?"

" Was Janet's—the Scotchwoman—*the murderess of Ellen !*"

.

CHAPTER IV.

PUSHING FORWARD.

THIS was unprepared for. A new element of
mystery in the story which had deepened, and the
threads of which were hard to follow. A stern
truth looming nearer to us, and casting all into a
darkness denser than before.

"Janet!" I repeated.

Much that had been incomprehensible in her
conduct flashed upon me after my brother's avowal; much that had seemed inconsistent with that
honesty of purpose in which my wife believed, recurred to me at once. Her seeming love for my
wife, and yet her refusal to leave Nettlewood
House and its master; Ellen's dislike to her, and

belief that she was a spy; her strangeness of demeanour; her persistent defence of Herbert Vaughan whenever attacked by me; the change that had come over her since Ellen's disappearance; the strange moods, irreconcilable with anything save the deep damning guilt of blood upon her hands.

I thought of her careful watch over my wife in the long illness that followed the mystery, and attributed her conduct then not so much to the love she experienced for Mary, as to the desire to stand between me and Mary's confession of the vileness of her brother's nature. I thought I saw all then clearly to the end; this woman had been Vaughan's tool, and obeyed his handiwork, or guessed at all that he had acted for himself. Ellen had seen her danger, and crossed the water by the private boat attached to Nettlewood House; Janet had flown to intercept her on her way through the Black Gap—a route better known to her than even to my sister.

"Have you anything more to tell me?"

"Very little. I was surprised at the action, but felt it unaccountable. I continued hidden, and watched her pass across the lake. When she took up the oar, she laid a pistol on the seat beside her.

Her face was like a ghost's—there was an awful
determination on it, in the moonlight. I saw her
row into the stream, the moon became hidden
again, and half way across the water, I lost sight
of her. Three quarters of an hour afterwards, I
heard the report of a pistol in the Black Gap
mountains. That's the story—what do you think
of it?"

"Did you watch for Janet's return?"

"Till the daylight came—then I gave her up."

"It is all incomprehensible to me," I muttered;
"the truth goes further away, and the mists of
which Ellen warned me close round me still more
densely."

"I am going at once to Nettlewood to prey on
Janet's fears. I think I may be able to learn
something from her—coming upon her by surprise."

"I have attempted to learn the truth from her
myself."

"Ah! but you have not had the same tools to
work with—leave it to me this time," he added,
with no little egotism.

"Meanwhile, I am to attempt Wenford with
Mary. Failing Wenford, I shall visit Vaughan."

"As you will," said Joseph reluctantly; "it

may be just possible to scare him away from his application for a divorce. If Janet confesses to anything, I shall telegraph to you—we may find another weapon to attack that scoundrel with."

"I would not have you build too much upon Janet."

"I shall take her off her guard."

I unlocked the door, evidently to Joseph's relief; he had never taken his eyes off me since my first exhibition of passion; he seemed to breathe freer when the door was opened.

"I—I hope you will do nothing hastily, Canute," he said almost imploringly. "I think, if we go cautiously to work, we shall catch my gentleman yet. Be careful with Wenford whilst I am away."

"And remember that we may be wrong concerning Janet," I said.

I remembered her past kindness to my wife before her marriage—all those little traits of character which showed her love and interest, and experienced a revulsion of feeling on the instant; I could not connect the disappearance of Ellen with any act of Janet Muckersie. And then there returned Joseph's story to me, and the light died out again.

Joseph took his departure after again warning me, and again inquiring at the street door whether I really thought it better to interfere with the first hearing of the divorce case.

"I should like to know how far he would go, Canute," he said, almost submissively.

"If that man·would repent at the eleventh hour, confess his sins and go his way, I could almost forgive him for my wife's sake," I replied.

"Ah! almost—not when you stood face to face with him at Ellen's grave?"

"No—not then!" I cried fiercely.

Joseph put up his umbrella and stepped into the wet streets. He went two or three steps away, and then returned before I had closed the door upon him.

"Canute," he said, in a changed voice, a voice more full of earnestness than I had listened to before in him, "you don't respect me much. You think I am all for money, and care little for poor Ellen. It isn't so—upon my soul, it isn't! I know the value of money, and have sinned for it —perhaps sold my soul to the devil for it, it is possible; but I always loved Ellen—she was my favourite of all of you."

He went away after that confession, and left me

looking after him, struggling with the wind and rain. I scarcely understood this sudden outburst of sympathy, after the careful fencing—the over-caution—that had preceded it. And yet I did not doubt its genuineness, for I did not believe in Joseph's power to feign a real emotion. At the last moment, parting from me to go on a long journey, the better nature which had rusted in him gave one little leap forward to show me that he was not wholly sordid, and that in the midst of much that was ignoble there was a grain or two of gold.

I returned to the room I had quitted, to find my wife anxiously expecting my return. She was looking very pale and agitated.

"What has happened afresh, Canute, dear?" she asked; "you are driving yourself wild again with this one awful thought. He has been here to disturb you once more."

"Mary, we are advancing swiftly to the truth, I hope. I must hope that, though your brother meet his fate with it."

"Canute, for my sake, I know that you will spare *him* when the time comes—that you will leave him to his God. I have been thinking of him so much lately," she added, "thinking that after all we may both be wrong in our estimation of his motives."

" He is a forger."

" Yes."

" You believe that he attempted your life once ?"

" Don't speak of the past. I have been all my life trying to shut it from me, Canute."

" You do not think that Ellen fled with Wenford ?"

" I do not."

" Then what is the mystery actuating every movement of your brother ? What reason for this cruel slandering of the dead—what wheel within a wheel slowly turning to our discomfiture and shame have we not a right to stop ?"

" You have heard more ?"

" Much that makes the mystery still difficult to solve. Mary, I have heard that Janet is implicated in my sister's disappearance."

" I will never believe it !" cried Mary, starting up. " Janet, my old nurse, my faithful friend, the shield between me and all the dangers that I feared once ! "

" She crossed the Ferry on that night Ellen disappeared—my brother saw her come down to the water's-edge, loose the boat, and push herself away from land."

"For what motive?" cried my wife.

"Mary, do you believe it possible that in her wild faithfulness for your brother, she would have sided with him against *her*? I have heard you say that she was a woman who would die for either of you, if need were ; is it possible that Ellen's life meant Herbert Vaughan's discomfiture, and that she spared it not when the hour came to act ?"

" No, no, I will not believe it !" cried Mary again; " all my life I have not been so deceived. Canúte, you and I will never be happy again until we know the truth, however hard or cruel. I see that now."

" Leave it to me."

"No !" she answered firmly, "I must work with you. You have thought to spare me by concealing, as far as possible, the troubles which perplexed you, but it was a kindness that kept my brain disturbed, and did no good to you. Let us attempt the truth together, and if it prove the vileness of those I love, or those in whom I have trusted, I will ask you at the last to be merciful for my sake. But you must trust in me utterly

now, and tell me all your sorrows. By sharing
them, I hope to lighten them eventually. Why,
Canute, I am stronger than you are now !"

It was the best plan after all. So I told her,
for the first time, the history of my struggles to
arrive at the secret of her brother's actions. I
spoke of my long search; of the evidence that
Ellen had been in the Black Gap Pass on the night
when it was stated she had fled with Wenford; I
related the particulars of Joseph Gear's plans; I
held nothing back. My wife and I faced the past
and gathered strength by being with each other,
and possessing no secrets from each other. In
keeping all that had perplexed me from her, I had
not acted wisely, when the time had passed in
which a shock might have robbed us of the hope
now hallowing our marriage. The child was born,
and I made my wife my confidante. I spoke of
Ellen boldly, and spared not her brother. Mary
was my second self, and it was strange to believe
in her power to strengthen me.

And I had not believed in vain; my own ap-
proximation to a mental prostration that had
alarmed her, brought her to my side, the com-
forter in whom I had had no trust till then. I
thought that my task was ever to comfort *her* by

my consoling words, to make her happy by treasuring within my own breast all things likely to disturb her; I had never pictured giving way myself, of the one idea becoming too heavy to withstand, and my requiring all her love and tenderness to keep me strong.

My weakness had dissipated hers; when there is danger to the loved one, the true woman steps forth to defend.

I told Mary of the discovery of Wenford's lodgings, possibly his hiding-place, and that method of action which Joseph Gear had suggested she considered best at once.

"Your brother is right," she said; "and although it is a weak hope, still it is the only one left us. We must seek the truth at all hazards for Ellen's sake—for yours. Let us go at once."

She was impatient to be enacting her own share in the search—for my sake now she would make every effort to arrive at the truth; for her sake, I was to be merciful to Herbert Vaughan or Janet, when the truth was facing us.

Leaving the child with my mother—ever the most careful of nurses—we set forth in a cab to Bermondsey. The rain was still steadily and heavily descending; from the sullen sky overhead

was to be read no augury of fine weather for some
time to come—people made the best of circumstances, and dashed through it, in lieu of loitering
under archways, door-portals, and shop-blinds.
New Road way, there were but few pedestrians in
the streets. Over the bridge, and making for
Bermondsey, the scene changed. In the poorer
world through which we were driven, the rain
seemed to have but little effect on the crowds of
people whom business had brought out that day;
women were chaffering at every corner, with other
women coolly seated in the rain at vegetable and
fish-stalls; lank, hungry-looking children raced
across the roadways, swam corks in the gutters,
sauntered about with bare feet on the wet pave-
ments, fought, screamed, and ran against people;
men out of work were smoking their pipes
composedly, with their backs against lamp-posts
or gin-shop doors; one man was striking at
his wife for trying to persuade him to come home;
a woman was being taken to the station-house for
filching bacon from a shop-board, and a mob of
sympathists was following her and her official
escort down the middle of the road, where the mud
was a foot deep.

"This is London indeed," whispered my wife,

drawing closer to me, with her old fear of things strange and new.

The cabman had some difficulty in finding the address which my brother had given me some time previously; but, by dint of many inquiries, we arrived at last before a row of one-storied brick houses, hemmed in by tan-pits and railway arches.

"This is Dynaston Street, sir."

"Stop at No. 10."

At No. 10 I sprang out, and announced my arrival at the door. A dirty-faced, slip-shod woman answered my summons thereat.

" Mr. Wenford is lodging here ? " I said.

" No, sir."

" No matter—a gentleman is lodging here whom I wish to see."

"Mr. Smith, do you mean, sir ? "

" Yes, Smith. A tall man, with——"

" With the ague—yes, sir, that's him. I'm a-going out marketing myself—will you please to shut the door when you leave him, and don't shut the string in, please, sir. He's in the upstairs front—I think he's expecting you."

" Indeed."

" He said a gentleman would very likely call

to-day to see him. You won't forget to shut the
door, and leave the string out, sir?"

And, with this last injunction, the lady of the
house, with her hair dishevelled, and her cap trail-
ing down her back, went out into the street, perfectly disregardful of the inclemency of the
weather.

I opened the cab-door, and assisted my wife to
alight. Perceiving that she had become very pale,
I asked her if she would leave the rest of the adventure to me.

" No, Canute," she replied, " I shall be strong
enough to face the worst. I am to act, not you,
remember; and I am only fearful of our meeting
Herbert here."

" We need not fear him if we do."

We closed the door after us, and went up a
flight of creaking stairs to the door of the front
room. Here I knocked, and here the well-known
voice—harsh and resonant as ever—called out,
" Come in."

I turned the handle of the door, and Mary and
I entered. A figure, very tall, but very wasted,
sat, or rather crouched, in an old-fashioned leathern chair, before a charcoal fire. A thin,
sallow face, half smothered by beard and mous-

tache, was turned towards the door as we entered; its whole expression changed to one of astonishment at our approach.

An oath escaped him in the first instance; he raised himself with some difficulty by pressing his hands on the elbows of the chair, stared at us, and then sat down again, with a half groan, and began to shiver violently.

"Who the devil would have thought to see you two here, in this house?" he said.

"Are we welcome, Mr. Wenford?" I asked.

"I can't say that you are. If you've come to pump anything from me—me who was always the hardest nut to crack in England—you're not welcome, and you've come a long distance out of your way for nothing."

"We came as friends, Mr. Wenford," remarked my wife; "we come for you to help us in a great distress."

He laughed hoarsely at this, and edged his chair nearer to the fire. He looked from me to her with some degree of interest, and then laughed and shivered again—ceasing his laugh to anathematize his shivering in the most forcible language.

"Say," he said, at last, "that you have come to rejoice over my downfall—to croak forth how

M 2

true the world was in its prophecy that Mad Wenford was going to the devil head-foremost. My
old father left me a fine fortune, and I threw it
all to the dogs—is that so odd a story in these
times, Gear?"

"Not very odd—but very pitiable."

"Stop that!" he shouted; "I always hated pity
in any shape or form; I always abominated a
fellow taking pity upon me. I was my own
master, and if I went the wrong way, why, I don't
know that there's any one to blame but myself.
Now, what do you two want here?"

"Cannot you guess?" I asked, sternly.

"I put a question—I don't want it stopped by
another—that's a trick I'm deep enough to see
through. Every cunning knave has had the idea
that I was mad enough to be duped, and I have
let them think so for my own purposes, sometimes,
and got the better of them in the long run. Now,
what do you want here?"

"Mr. Wenford," said my wife, approaching
him, and holding forth her hand, "you and I, at
least, have been always friends."

"Ah! we might have been more than friends
once, if that fellow hadn't turned up," pointing to
me.

"Say that we are friends still—that you, who once wished me every peace and happiness, will not, by your silence, wreck them both, sir?"

"Are *you* unhappy?" he asked, wonderingly.

"My husband's life is mine, and his is one distracted by a great fear. I am unhappy to think that his name should be dishonoured, that his sister—sleeping in her grave, sir—should not be spared the foulest of all calumnies that can disgrace a woman."

"Sleeping in her grave?" he repeated; "who says that, now?"

"I say it."

"I am never to know all," he muttered; "I am to be told just as much as seems sufficient for some purpose or other, which is not explained to me. When did she die?"

"She was murdered on the night you and James Baines went through the Triesdale Pass," I answered.

He started, but made no response. My presence there was objectionable to him; I was associated with his greatest disappointment, and in his low estate he loved me none the better. Before he turned his face away from me, I saw hate and anger in his deep-set eyes.

" What does he mean about murdered, Mary Gear?" he asked.

" You know of whom we are talking?"

He nodded.

" Ellen—my brother's wife."

" Yes."

She disappeared on the same night that you left Nettlewood; her flight was coupled with that of yours—your names are still mentioned together as a guilty couple who betrayed my brother's honour."

He lay back in his chair and shivered more and more. The ague-fit was on him, and he could not hold a limb still.

" I know all this," he gasped, " it's no news to me."

" Will you, in remembrance of the better times when you professed a love for me," urged my wife, " confirm our suspicions that Mrs. Vaughan did not fly with you to New York—did not in any way deserve the foul names bestowed upon her? Are you, a gentleman—a man well born, well educated—so lost to all sense of what is right or just, as to let the lie go further, defaming you as well as her—have you so altered, Wenford, as to be bribed to such a cruel infamy—you I respected, almost loved, once!"

., "Say that again!" he cried, his eyes lighting up, his wild face all aglow at her assertion.

"Wenford, let me tell you that truth, of which my husband is aware—which I am not ashamed to own. Years ago, when you asked me to be your wife, I was miserable and unhappy, and only you pitied that unhappiness and loved me for it. For that I almost loved you in return—had you been a man to whom I could have trusted my future, I should have married you."

"You would have committed suicide," he answered; "after all, it was better that I lost you, though you were the one chance to make me a good man, and it went by and left me what I am. This is a wreck enough, Mrs. Gear—moral enough for any canting story-book."

"I am sorry to see you thus reduced."

"You had always a feeling heart. Thank you."

"But I should hate and despise you, if it were a truth that you were reduced to that infamy with which the world would brand you. Wenford, I believe better of you than that; I ask you to strengthen me in that belief."

"For *his* sake?" with a half-glance towards me.

"No, for mine."

"It is better to say nothing," he said, after a visible struggle to resist that last appeal; "I can say nothing to make you more happy. I am a coward, who has consented to play the villain's part —what does it matter," with a stamp of his foot, "what I do now?"

"You are the dupe of a man more cunning than yourself! All his life you have been a slave to him."

"It suits my purpose now at least.. How horribly cold it is!—what an unearthly noise the rain makes beating against the glass!"

"Then you will tell me nothing, Wenford?"

"I can tell you nothing that will make your heart more light," he answered, "so I will keep my own counsel. Please go now, you're like a spirit to me, and freeze every drop of blood in my veins. I daren't look at you again."

"Wenford, will you let me be the judge of what is good or bad news to me. Rather than you keep a cruel silence, I will go down on my knees and beg you to speak out."

"No—don't do that!" he cried, tottering to his feet with undisguised alarm; "I'm only a child now, and you'll floor me completely if you do that."

"You wish this divorce case to proceed—you will not defend your own name, but for a bribe let the honest world scout you in the streets."

"For a bribe!" he shouted, then dropped into the chair again, and covered his face with his hands; "well, yes, yes—it's as bad as that!"

"You confess it."

"You wish to stop this case for your husband's sister's sake. By some unaccountable means you have found me out to tell me *this!*"

"Yes."

"But if it be for the best that the case proceeds and sets your sister free? If it be your sister's wish to take her share of disgrace, rather than be tied to Herbert Vaughan for life?"

"If it were true, I would still wish to stay it—but if she were living and acting for such a purpose, I would despise her," cried Mary; "Edmund Wenford, can you swear to me that Ellen lives?"

"I have *his* word for it."

"Do you believe that she of all women would consent to this odious compact? Are you so much my brother's slave as to be blinded by this vile falsehood?"

" Well—it never struck me—I have not seen it in that light. If that Vaughan has again thrown dust in my eyes, I'll—I'll—"

He paused to struggle with his ague-fit, and pointed with his trembling hand to a glass containing some liquor on the mantel-piece. Mary reached it, and held it to his lips.

After a while he was more composed; more like his old self. There was a sternness about his brows which showed the man strong to resist yet.

" If he be trying to deceive me—hiding me here, while he works on and fears no opposition—I may turn on him at the last. Sit down here, and tell me your story, beginning from the date of my escape from Nettlewood."

Mary did so, and he sat and listened patiently, taking no heed of me, a watcher of this strange interview. When I once broke in to correct some little error of statement into which my wife had unwittingly fallen, he fiercely bade me be silent.

Mary related how the first news of the alleged elopement was brought to her, and by what bearer; spoke of the letter which Wenford had written to her brother, and which he read that morning of the discovery—of my long search and her illness, of my tracking him to Liverpool, of the many reasons which we both had for believing Ellen had come to an untimely end.

Wenford was silent till the last words had escaped my wife's lips, then he dashed his hand upon the leathern chair-arm with a violence which startled both of us.

"If he had been true to me, if he had kept faith with me, I would have gone side by side with him in his villainy to the last—but I will stand no more of it! I trusted in him, and he deceived me —gaining his ends, I can see that he will throw me off, and deceive me again! Mr. Gear," turning to me for the first time, "I have been a miserable villain all my life, but not the wretch that he would make me out. Hasty and reckless, but not crafty and subtle. I did not elope with your sister."

"I knew it—I was sure of it."

"I did not know that it was intended that the world should think so, until I was back in London two months since—I knew nothing of your sister, or of his plans concerning her and me, until I came back penniless and ague-stricken to London."

"But that letter which you wrote to Vaughan on the night of your flight."

"Do you remember the words?"

"All of them."

"Will you repeat them?"

I repeated them at his request. Every word of
his letter, like every word of that epistle falsely
attributed to Ellen, had been burned into my
memory. I had no need to ask for the copies
Vaughan had promised me.

" 'Forgive me and my betrayal of a trust,' your
letter began," I quoted, " 'but the tide's too strong
for me. For the sake of our old friendship, I have
fought an unequal fight and am vanquished. I
am really Mad Wenford now—to all intents and
purposes as raving mad as any lunatic from Han-
well. Ellen accompanies me. NED WENFORD.' "

"I see—I see!" cried Wenford, when I had
concluded; "yes, I am no match for Herbert
Vaughan—his cunning is Satanic. I wrote that
letter at his dictation, barring the words 'Ellen
accompanies me,'—he put them in afterwards, to
further his own purposes. Now let me own what
a villain I am."

He seemed to struggle with a threatened return
of his ague, and to master it. He addressed himself to me now, and my wife sat at his side, pale
and anxious, and unremarked by him. He would
not own to her what a villain he had been!

"He and I went partners in a mine, by way of a last dash for riches, ere we were both reduced to beggary. The mine was a failure, and the creditors were ready to swoop down upon us both. There were left some thousands at the bankers, and he persuaded me to let the world suppose I had suddenly decamped with them, foreseeing the ruin there was in store for us. That would leave a large amount of money less for the creditors, and on the night of Mrs. Ray's ball we shared that amount, and I wrote the letter exculpating him. He worded it so that it should refer to Ellen, and so played a double game, in which that two-faced knave, Jem Baines, assisted him. We left Liverpool for New York on the 24th of July."

"And the woman calling herself Ellen Vaughan who sailed by that ship?"

"A woman picked up at Liverpool by Baines, and paid to take her passage out in your sister's name. She was thrown in my way during the voyage—but only by Baines' own confession has the truth lately come to my knowledge."

"Why have you returned to England?"

"I spent my money—squandered it after the old fashion, and then returned, simply for the reason that I was tired of America. When I

came back here, I discovered the plot, and went in
search of Herbert Vaughan, who had been very busy
during my absence.   Then the explanation came ;
it had been Ellen's wish to separate from her husband; they had planned between them the scheme,
which Vaughan confided to me.   Ellen had flirted
with me at Nettlewood to give a colour to the story,
it was said; she left Nettlewood on the same night as
myself, to make the end more credible; she is
willing to lose her good name rather than be in his
power ever again.   Vaughan is anxious to marry
Letty Ray, from whose fortune I am to receive
ten thousand pounds, the price of my silence in
this matter.   James Baines is to be the witness
ready to swear that he accompanied us to America.
And all this is not arranged between man and
wife, you believe?"

"I believe it firmly."

"I thought it was his wife's wish as well as his
—I had heard of such cases before, and had become
too much of a wretch to be shocked at this one—
there was money to be earned by keeping silent,
and the thought of murder never crossed me for a
moment.   Even now," he added dubiously,
"Herbert Vaughan's story is more feasible than

yours—only, only, there *was* a look in Mrs. Vaughan that was above all this."

" Above it—yes."

" And I never made war against a woman— damn it, I never plotted against a woman's happiness in my life—I was never so bad as that, after all !"

He turned quite proudly towards my wife, as though that assertion extenuated all the evil of which he had been guilty.

" I thought it all had been arranged, and was better for all parties concerned—but if it has not been arranged, then," sinking his voice, " there has been foul play, and I have done with Herbert Vaughan. Scamp as I am, there is a line at which even *I* stop. The more I think of it," he added, his brow contracting, " the more I see what a madman I am to let that man have the handling of my name, and keep his own so pure before the world. Why, the Wenfords were always the best family—he is only the son of a solicitor !"

It was pitiful boasting, at which he laughed hollowly the moment afterwards. The mockery of this poor pride struck home even to him.

"I'll not say anything more against him," he said after a pause, during which he had begun to tremble violently again, "I'll hold my own and stand my ground now. I don't know by facts whether he or you are right, but if he do not give you his wife's address, or send it to me by your hands, within six hours from your meeting with him, I defend my case as co-respondent in the Divorce Court. By ——!" he took an awful oath here, "that will startle him somewhat, and foil him with his own weapons. A good scheme—a good scheme!"

"He may seek you out, and try to explain it— he may impose upon you again."

"He will be here presently—he promised me to call this morning at eleven."

"It is past one."

"Ah! he will not come then—he hangs back, and don't like too many questions asked. He is putting me off, and every day is of moment to us. When is the case announced for hearing?"

"In four days' time."

"I will leave here at once, and alarm him by my disappearance. Why shouldn't I try his nerves a little, as he has tried mine? Where shall I go?"

"We will find you a lodging adjacent to our house in the New Road."

"Don't let him know where I am—if that man were driven to bay, I wouldn't answer for my life. I'm not so strong as I used to be, and this is an ugly neighbourhood."

The new fear appeared to unnerve him; he sat and struggled with his weakness. Looking at him helpless and trembling there, I could scarce believe this was the fierce iron-hearted being I had known at Nettlewood. He had appeared much changed when we first came upon him in his miserable lodging; now that he had lost all confidence in Vaughan, and was impressed by a belief in Ellen's death, he was but the shadow of his former self— bewildered by all that we and he had attempted to explain. And after all, the clouds were still as dense, and Ellen still as far away! Before us only lay the chance of adjourning or defending the divorce case—of scaring Herbert Vaughan from his secure position, and keeping Ellen's name still spotless. Wenford was anxious to begone— to accompany us at once.

"It's bad weather for me to be out, but I can't stop here—I won't stop here any longer. Let us go at once, before my resolution gives way. I was always Mad Wenford, never in one mood ten minutes together.   What a life mine has been!"

He was becoming childish, or the medicine on the mantel-piece was powerful, and affected his head a little.

"Who attends you for the ague?" I asked, almost involuntarily.

"Not Herbert Vaughan," he said, quickly enough; "no, no!" with a laugh, "his friends die much too suddenly for me!"

. He noticed my wife's hand suddenly press itself to her heart, and he said, with some of that gentlemanly courtesy which he had exhibited more than once in the past days:

"Pardon me, Mrs. Gear—but I did not mean to pain you."

We went out of the room together—I, wondering at the many changes in his moods which he had exhibited during the interview, and fearing that from his natural instability all might yet be marred. I was anxious to lure him from that house, and startle his accomplice by his disappearance. It would be one great step gained on our side, at least—and Vaughan had held the winning hand till then.

"Is there any money owing to the landlady?"

"No—I pay her in advance."

"Are you in want of money?"

"When I am, I may ask you," he said, with his old bluntness.

He tottered about the room like an old man, collecting a few scraps of wearing apparel together from a chest of drawers in one corner of the room, and crowding them into a portmanteau, which his shaking fingers were unable to lock. He was ready at last, shrouded to the eyes in a thick heavy cloak.

We descended the stairs—the house was still empty—the cabman tired of waiting on the box in the rain, had got into his vehicle and fallen fast asleep there. He emerged from the cab at our request, and mounted the box; I closed the street-door after us, and left the string outside as the landlady had requested; we entered the cab, and were driven back towards the New Road.

Crossing one of the crowded Bermondsey thoroughfares, we were detained a moment by a street-fight, and a mob of excited lookers-on. I glanced from the window for an instant, and saw James Baines standing a little aloof, and deeply interested in the proceedings. That street-fight

N 2

had saved us, perhaps, for as I watched I saw
Baines suddenly turn away and proceed at a very
rapid pace in the direction of the house we had
quitted.

CHAPTER V.

WATCHING AND COUNTER-WATCHING.

HAVING safely placed Mad Wenford in lodgings contiguous to our own, and seen to those common comforts, which, from choice or necessity, he appeared to have denied himself, it was left me to still further prosecute my plans for arresting the progress of the divorce case. There was at least the hope of gaining time, which was valuable now to Ellen's fame.

I was anxious to proceed at once to Vaughan's house in London, but Mary was also anxious concerning me, and begged me to do nothing rashly. The impulse had been given me to proceed again, and every minute lost was to be regretted by me.

I could scarcely eat the dinner which Mary's thoughtfulness insisted upon placing before me, ere I ventured forth, strong in my new hope to baffle Vaughan.

Mary would, have accompanied me, but I was firm in my resolution to undertake this part of my task alone. All that I wished to say to her brother was better without her presence as a witness. She had fulfilled a fair share of work that day; furthermore, she had risked her health in venturing forth in this inclement weather.

It was five o'clock when I was ready to depart; the night was coming on, and the rain was still descending heavily.

"I cannot bear you out of my sight, Canute," she urged. "You promised me that we should work together from this time forth."

"Ever together, Mary, sharing one common trouble," I answered; "but to-night your post is here. There is nothing gained, and only your brother put more upon his guard by your presence at my side. We must never be both absent from home, now Wenford is so near us."

She let me go my way reluctantly; her fear of me had not yet abated; the one idea that drove me forwards was less to be fought against than ever. But I had grown stronger with it; further proof of all that I had hitherto but guessed at, had braced my nerves to go on to the end, fearing no break down by the way. I saw the end looming before me, dark and horrible, and the full light of day upon the ghastly mystery; my near approach gave me an unnatural courage, which I felt would not die out until Vaughan or I remained the victor. Afterwards the re-action might test my strength more forcibly, but the worst would have been faced, and I should have done my duty to one hidden securely from me now.

"I may be late—don't sit up," were my last injunctions to Mary, who parted from me with a wistful look.

"You will be careful—you will keep ever on your guard, Canute?"

"Trust me."

So we parted, and I proceeded through the rain and wind to the residence of Herbert Vaughan. I preferred to walk every step of the way to the West-end hotel at which my brother-in-law was residing for a time, and the address of which had been furnished me by Wenford. Though the night was stormy and dark, I preferred walking onwards at a rapid pace; I could not sit still, and

let a host of thoughts bewilder me—I must hurry
on with it, and keep in action, for my brain's sake.
Strong and energetic as I felt, I was less calm;
sitting for five minutes motionless, disturbed me.
I was impelled onwards by a force that I was
powerless to cope with—the force that rendered
rest a misery to me.

I reached the hotel, and was informed that Mr.
Vaughan had been absent about an hour. Did
anyone know when he would return? The porter
thought not, but would inquire of Mr. Vaughan's
valet. Mr. Vaughan's valet made his appearance
after a while—a sleek-faced, straight-haired, young
man, whom I had not seen before.

" Did I wish to see Mr. Vaughan very particularly ? "

" Very particularly indeed."

" Should I excuse him, but he had only been in
Mr. Vaughan's service two days, and was going
down to Nettlewood with him presently. Was my
name Wenford ? "

I nodded my head. The man brightened up at
once.

"Mr. Vaughan wished to see Mr. Wenford
very particularly. Would Mr. Wenford wait in
his apartments till his return, or, if pressed for

time, ask for him · of the box-keeper at the Hay-
market Theatre ? "

"I am pressed for time—I will follow Mr.
Vaughan."

The valet bowed, and looked vacantly after me.
The porter opened the swing glass entrance doors,
and bowed me down the great stone flight of steps ;
I went on in the wind and rain to the theatre,
where this man could find the will and heart
to go.

To the box-entrance, where I inquired if a Mr.
Vaughan had left any directions as to the number
of his box. Mr. Vaughan had taken a private
box yesterday, and was then in the house. Did I
wish to see him ? Presently. I took a ticket for
the first tier, and presented myself in the lobby
for admittance. The box-keeper looked very dubiously at my muddy trousers and boots, and was
evidently far from struck with the eligibility of
my claims for admittance.

"Put me in a back seat for a moment. I am
not going to stop," I said.

"Back seat—yes, sir—thank you."

Relieved in his mind, the box-keeper opened the
door, and indicated a seat at the back of the dress-
circle. The audience was absorbed in the per-

formance on the stage, and my appearance, soiled
and disreputable as it was, did not attract any
attention. I took my seat, and looked round the
first tier ; in a private box near the stage was the
object of my search—the man who had so influ-
enced my life. He was seated between two ladies
—the one in black silk on his right hand, with the
scarlet wreath crossing her raven hair, there
was no difficulty in recognizing as Letty Ray,
much as she had altered since my first acquaintance with her. On his left was the lady who had
acted as governess to Letty, and was still resident
with her as companion.

Herbert Vaughan seemed in good spirits; the
disappearance of Wenford did not apparently
affect him much, or rouse greatly his suspicions.
Probably he knew by this time that a lady and
gentleman had called for Wenford in his miserable
lodgings, and taken him away with them ; and it
was not difficult to guess who were likely to be the
agents in that affair. If he were perplexed by our
conduct, he bore his embarrassment well, and was
at his ease at that moment by the side of the heiress,
whose fortune he coveted. I felt a grim satisfaction in sitting there unperceived—an opponent
advancing to make one last desperate effort to

thwart all the evil he had planned. Life had flown smoothly on with him, and he had planned and plotted with but little opposition—in his dark career he had found many tools; at every turn of the road came friends to trust him, and believe in him.

Sitting there facing me, it was difficult to think him a villain even then; his whole appearance was deceptive. A fair-haired handsome man, clever and accomplished, with the gift of winning hearts by the same manners which were as false as he, and hid so much that was foully treacherous.

He sat there by Miss Ray's side, her acknowledged lover, ere the links that bound him to another had ostensibly been broken; and she, whose latter-day studies should have taught her better, saw neither the boldness nor the shame of it. He was paying more attention to her than to the performance on the stage, and her interest was for him, not for the sparkling comedy which had crowded the house that night. All her life had been spent in loving Vaughan; she had vowed to love him in the face of a treachery that should have set him far apart from her for ever. I believed that nothing which the world could say would ever have power to wean her from him.

Whence arose this man's influence over the female
heart—this fascination, as it were, of his serpent's
glance? It had never affected me; in the early
days before I knew the evil at his heart, I had dis-
trusted him; and yet my sister Ellen, a girl not
easily deceived, quick to detect the real from the
false, was taken in the toils, and thus made the
one great error of her life. Looking at him then,
watching every movement as he sat there, I could
believe that he was less an actor than a man who
lost all consciousness of himself in the object of the
present hour. It was not acting; it was reality.
It had been his business to fall in love with Letty
Ray, and for the time it *was* love—the same love
which, in its fervour and passing truth, had deceived so cruelly his wife. In that hour, he thought
no more of his victim, or of the blood upon his head
—no matter whether Ellen were slain by his hand,
or Janet Muckersie's. He was a man who framed
a purpose for his own advancement, his own security—and then dashed at it, caring not for law or
human life. The time was coming to meet him on
the road he was pursuing, and do my best to baffle
him. He or I must surely fall in the time but a
little distant from us both.

I left the box as the act-drop descended, and

made my way to the other side of the house, in search of the box-keeper. I was forestalled in my search by Vaughan himself, who came rapidly along the lobby, and would have passed me had I not caught his arm.

"Mr. Vaughan, I am in search of you."

He compressed his lips together—the only sign of being taken by surprise.

"We meet at strange times, and in strange places, Mr. Gear," he said; "you will excuse me, but I have a friend to visit in the dress-circle, and cannot stop an instant now."

"I have spent much time in searching for you, and my business is important."

"This is no place for important business," he said, coldly; "call at my hotel in the morning.'

"I wish to speak of the divorce you are anxious to obtain."

"I will not speak of it to *you*," he said, fiercely.

"It must be stopped."

"There is no power on earth or in heaven to stop it," he cried; "I tell you I have willed it. Let me pass."

"I have been slowly gathering my proofs together, Mr. Vaughan—I do not believe that you dare to face them at the last. I wish to speak of

those proofs, and to warn you that you are court-
ing your own destruction by following this scheme
to the end."

"If you have anything to say to me, or warn
me of, call at the hotel in the morning. I promise
you to hear all that you have to tell me then—I
swear that I will not listen to a word more here!
You have tracked me like a hound, you have set
spies upon my path, you have sought, by every
petty meanness, to fasten a great crime upon me;
you have lured away this very day Ellen's accomplice to tamper with—you are my enemy!"

"Be it so—your enemy if you will. You were
my sister's—I accept the name."

"I will see you to-morrow. Candidly, I am
anxious to see you—to know what I have to face,
and to warn you of all that may overwhelm you if
you stand longer in my path. I will be at home
to-morrow morning at ten."

"At ten—I will be there."

I saw that it was useless to continue the conversation there, and I saw that he would keep his
word and meet me. Our altercation in the box
lobby had already turned more than one wondering pair of eyes towards us, and he had raised his
voice as if for the purpose of attracting undue

attention. I knew that time was valuable to him —that in four days the trial of Ellen's honour would occur, but I felt that I could afford to wait till the morning rather than attempt an explanation in the theatre. I had not proof enough yet to break through his net of circumstance, and I scarcely dared defy him. If he would listen patiently to me, I might, by cautious fencing, arouse his fears, and make him pause awhile. I wanted time, for I felt that with it would come back Ellen's innocence to me.

He left me, and I went immediately out of the theatre, where the wind and the rain met me with their old violence. A terrible night for those afoot; such a night as I scarcely remembered before that time, and only equalled by the nights which followed it. For the wet was of long continuance, and night and day for the greater part of that week, kept steadily and unceasingly on, till people despaired of the sunshine ever again.

I walked home. My head ached and my blood was at fever heat; the rain that dashed upon me came as a relief, and I feared no danger from it. The squares and streets I crossed in my passage to the New Road were almost deserted that night; now and then a man or woman, cowering under

an umbrella, flitted by me; once a drunken woman
asked me for alms from the shadow of a doorway;
occasionally a policeman in oil-skin cape and great-
coat, gruffly bade me good-night, or looked suspi-
ciously after me, according to the impression my
appearance made upon him.

In the New Road at last, and thinking of
Mary's face brightening up at my early return.
She was anxious about me; she had grave fears
for my health; out of her sight, and to her nervous
mind, I was in the, midst of danger which might
strike me down—it was pleasant to think of her
welcome leap towards me when I stood once more
in the house which we had christened home for the
nonce. I had walked on the opposite side of the
way, intending to look in upon Wenford, whose
apartments almost faced my own, before proceeding home. This intention I changed when it recurred to me that Vaughan had already guessed
that I had discovered Wenford, and might have
possibly set his emissaries to watch my house and
neighbourhood. For the present, and until I had
had an interview with Vaughan, perhaps it was
best that I should not visit Wenford. I passed by
the house and went on, looking across the wide
road towards the lighted blind at which I should

not have been surprised to find drawn aside, and Mary at her post there, waiting in the hope of seeing me pass the last gas lamp on the opposite side of the way. But no one was there; it was not ten o'clock, and I had given no hope of my return before that hour.

I was preparing to cross the road, when I became aware of a figure standing in the deep recess of the doorway of my house, standing back in the shadow, where no light could fall upon it. It was possible that it was some straggler seeking shelter from the rain; but it had rained pitilessly all day, and there was little chance of its abatement. I was suspicious; there were valid reasons for a watch being set upon the house, and all that issued thence; it was imperative, in the midst of danger, to be constantly on guard. I passed rapidly by on the other side of the way, and went on for a hundred yards or more, crossing the road suddenly, and turning back again. I reached my own door, and passed by—the figure was gone, and the deep recess of the doorway was untenanted.

No one had passed me, so the watcher, or loiterer, must have proceeded down the road. I walked rapidly onwards, but overtook no one; at the corner of the first street, I paused—all was

deserted there: far ahead of me gleamed the wet
deserted pavement; on either side of the way
there was not a human being visible.

I was at a loss to account for this, until the
natural idea suggested itself that it was a mes-
senger or visitor to the landlady, and that during
the time of my passing the house for the first
time, and that of my return to it, he or she had
been admitted. I was becoming nervous myself,
fancying that the world was full of spies, and
every little incident had some hidden meaning
which threatened shipwreck to my peace of mind.
I returned, opened the door by means of the latch-
key which had been furnished me—and went up-
stairs towards the front room.

There was the murmur of voices inside; the voice
of Mary, and another voice that was not strange to
me, and was not my mother's. I turned the handle
of the door, and entered suddenly. A tall woman,
thickly shawled and veiled, rose from the chair in
which she had been seated, and stood with one
large red hand clutching the back, and looking
nervously towards me.

"Measter Gear!"

"Janet!"

CHAPTER VI.

GUILTY OR NOT GUILTY?

I advanced towards Janet with extended hands. All my doubts of her seemed to vanish away in her presence.

"I am glad that you have come to help us at last, Janet. We have been sorely tried."

"I ha'e na coom to help ye," she responded, gloomily, "ony to make sure that the lassie war well, and na gieing wa' agin."

"For no other purpose?"

"For nane ither."

"A strange purpose to come from Nettlewood," I said, doubtfully.

"Mayhap it be," was the short reply; "ye who

ne'er anderstood me, may hae sic thochts—I canna help them—they are na beesiness o' mine."

She still clutched tenaciously at the back of the chair, and did not look into my face. Through the thick veil she wore I could see that she was very wan and haggard, like a woman who had been sorely tried by trouble.

"Janet," I said, after a pause, "lately we have heard strange tales of you. In the search that we are still making for my lost sister, your name has crossed us to harass and perplex us more —to confound still further the mystery on which so little light has fallen."

"Ye suspected me."

"Your actions have been unaccountable, and are therefore naturally suspicious."

"So she saes," replied Janet, with an angry gesture of her hand towards my wife; "she—that ye ha' turned agin me at the last: she, that I ha' lo'ed sae weel, and streeven sae hard for. Measter Gear, ye might ha' waited. In gude time, I might ha' coom to ye, jist as now, and ha' told ye a' I kenned, which be na' sae much as ye expect, may-hap. But the time be na' yet, and I am seelent as the grave."

She closed her lips together, and leaned heavily

upon the chair back till it cracked again. She was firm and inflexible, troubled though she was.

"Janet," said my wife, advancing to her, and seeking to take her hand, which was instantly hidden beneath her shawl; "in my heart I do not suspect you—in my heart, I love you as faithfully as ever. I have only asked you to help us in our dire distress—for my husband's sake rather than for mine."

"I ha' coom here the nicht to ask ye to wait for the time when I can speak a' the awfu news which chokes my heart oop, and ye wull not wait. Ye turn agin me, I who would ha' deed for ye, ower and ower agin, Mary Gear."

"Janet," I said sternly, "this is no time for waiting. The days are hurrying on, and every moment that keeps us from the truth is death to the honest name my sister has a claim to."

"Ye ha' doon na' gude—ye ha' set spies upon ye by yer restlessness—I warn ye even noo tó seet doon patient and let things tak their coorse —there's na better wa' left for ye baith, if ye'll tak an auld woman's word for it. Oh! sir, if ye'll ony keep still e'en noo!"

The woman flung up her veil as if for air, and looked earnestly and beseechingly towards me. She had changed so much since we had seen her last, that at her wan face Mary and I both started back. This new manner, this excitement following so closely upon her former stoicism, or obduracy, seemed to betray her more, and show more clearly to me where my suspicions should have been directed long since. We were hurrying on to the truth, and she was shrinking from it—her guilty conscience had brought her from Cumberland to face us.

"Janet, you would deceive us," I said, sternly; "you would throw us off our guard at the eleventh hour, when the chances are in our favour. I will listen to no advice from one who played her part in the past tragedy, and sought to turn us from our search by seeming ignorance."

"What part ha' I played?"

"Janet Muckersie," I said firmly; "on the night that my sister disappeared, you crossed Nettlewood Ferry. You were seen to steal down in the dead of night and make your way across to the other side to intercept—as I fully believe you *did* intercept—my poor sister hurrying away from the danger of which God had warned her."

Janet's right hand joined her left on the chair-back, her figure appeared to sway uneasily, and

be supported only by the firm clutch she retained
there. More and more ghastly that strangely-
marked face turned; it became still more a difficulty to breathe.

" Who told ye this ?"

" You were seen to place a pistol by your side—
a pistol-shot was fired in the Black Gap at twenty-
five minutes past two—you returned back to
Nettlewood House by the private boat, by which
Ellen had fled at an earlier period, and your
master, the prime mover, for whom you have sacrificed all chance of Heaven, began those plans of
infamy, by which he vainly sought to throw dust
in the world's eyes, and screen himself and
you."

" My God! how did ye ken a' this ?"

She sank slowly into the chair against which
she had supported herself, and with her feverish
hands unfastened the strings of her bonnet.

" Gie me some water—I shall dee else !"

There was a caraffe on the supper-table ; Mary
ran to it, poured out a glass of water, and held it
to the lips of the astonished woman. When Janet
had drunk some of the water, she appeared to
revive somewhat. She pushed a long grey lock of
hair that had trailed forward beneath her bonnet

again, and gathered her shawl more closely round
her form.

"Why did I coom here this nicht again my
ain sense that told me it were wrong?" she muttered.

"Janet," whispered my wife, who was still leaning over her, "will you not deny or explain this?
Will you not, for the sake of the old times when
you were like a mother unto me, and took the
place of mother, loving me and guarding me from
evil, tell all now? If for the sake of him who
stood even nearer to your heart than I, you have
been led on, God knows by what specious argument, or by what awful threats, to take poor Ellen's
life, will you not confess all the temptations which
bewildered you, and the story which has ended for
us all so terribly?"

The white lips parted after a struggle to speak.

"Na," was the hollow, almost the despairing
answer.

"Janet, your old love for me—that past faithfulness which stood my friend and shielded me
from danger—stands now between me and my
judgment of you. Neither my husband nor myself talk of vengeance for the crime into which
you may have been led, we only ask you for the

truth, and if you will trust in our mercy—if you
will only trust in me to plead with Canute for
you!"

"I ask ye ony to let me gae noo. I canna do or
sae anythin'; I'm a woman with my speerit wholly
bracken. I ha' na confeedence in ane sool in the
world—the whole world turns agin me in my
trooble."

"Janet, you have said too much," I exclaimed;
"I cannot let you leave us without an explanation.
If you be obstinate with me, I must be stern with
you. You are the possessor of an awful secret,
and I *must* have it!"

"I am in yer power—I ha' coom o' my ain free
wull to place mysel' in it, and ye can hauld me in
the trap, gin it please ye," she replied, more
sullenly.

There was a painful interim of silence. It was
a difficult step how to proceed; there was no
wringing the secret from her, when she had vowed
herself to silence; had I been disposed to hand
her over to the custody of the law, it was difficult to
say if my charge against her could have been for
an instant entertained.

And amidst all this, was the doubt as to whether
she were really guilty; the doubt which, despite

that strange bewildered demeanour, would assert
itself, and remind me and Mary of many traits of
character so wholly different from a remorseless
and conscienceless woman.   And yet, that demeanour might be an evidence of guilt, which might
also represent her old desire to stand the friend of
Herbert Vaughan, and screen him, at her
own, or any cost, from the consequences of his
crime.

She dropped down into the chair, on the back
of which she had been leaning, and clasped her
bony hands together. If I had thundered forth,
" Janet Muckersie, I arrest you on the charge of
wilful murder!" she could not have more completely given up, or looked more prepared for the
worst.

My wife said " Janet" to her, in a low voice
again, but she took no heed; her eyes were steadily
fixed upon the carpet at her feet, wherein her
future destiny might have been written, so intently was her gaze directed to it.

The position was intricate, and hard to fight
one's way through; in the chequered ground before us what was to be the next step ? I had
spoken firmly; and had determined even on a
sternness of procedure, but the way was dark

enough, and I had little hope of influencing Janet. The silence in that room was very painful; the clock on the mantel-piece ticked unnaturally loud; my mother's footsteps overhead appeared to shake the house.

I looked towards my wife, whose eyes had long been anxiously directed towards me. She motioned me to cross the room to her.

"Canute," she whispered, when I was at her side, "what is to be done with her? She will say nothing—you might kill her, but you could never induce her to divulge a secret which she considered it her duty to keep. Canute, for *his* sake, not for her own, she will remain for ever silent."

"I am sorry," I said, firmly, "but I must not spare her."

"What will you do?"

"I am undecided yet—all is mystery still beyond the present moment."

"Canute, will you let poor Janet go her way?" she entreated. "In my heart still I do not think her guilty; and she has come of her own free will to see me."

"Or to spy upon us both, and see how near we are drawing to the truth."

"No, no, Canute. You are hard and uncharitable."

"She—ah!"

I wrenched my arm away from the hand that had been lightly laid upon it, and dashed towards Janet. But she had been too quick for me —with one sudden spring she had leaped from the chair to the door, passed through into the passage, and drawn the door after her, retaining her hold upon the handle. The strong grip of the Scotchwoman was too much for me, she held the door to despite my efforts to wrench it open. A moment afterwards the key, which was outside, turned in the lock, and we were prisoners in our turn.

"Locked in!" I cried, running towards the window—struggling with the blind and window catch—with everything just then that seemed to get in my way and delay me. I flung up the window, and my wife screamed, and threw her arms around me—the wind and the rain came driving in again; with a crash that echoed through the house, the table-lamp was blown over, extinguished, and broken.

I looked out as the street-door opened, and Janet came hurrying forth—a figure of guilt, full of fear for the danger into which she had thrust herself. Had my wife's arms not been round me, I should have leaped on to the pavement, so void of reflection had I become.

"Canute—Canute—for my sake!" she entreated.

The streets were deserted—along the long line of pavement on which the rain was rattling fiercely still, there fell not the shadow of one single human being—escape she must.

"Stop that woman!" I shouted forth into the darkness, but no one responded to my call, and Janet swiftly and decisively hurried away, and the instant afterwards was lost to me.

I shouted forth again into the night, and only the echoes lurking amongst the opposite houses answered me. At the same moment my mother unlocked the door, and stood amazed at the darkness, and at the rush of air that made towards her.

"Mercy on me!—what's the matter?"

I remembered that she had hopes of Ellen's life still—and that my thoughts had never darkened hers. I closed the window, and sat down. I felt that it was hopeless to follow Janet then.

"What's the matter?" repeated my mother.

"Nothing," I answered, "only a bad character

forcing her way into the house, and locking us in. She has gone now."

"Ah! there's a good many bad characters about. Let us look round and see there's nothing missing."

CHAPTER VII.

A TELEGRAM.

HURRIED on by the one desire to be stirring in
my sister's cause; excited by the progress of every
hour that brought the trial of her woman's
honesty more near to me; conscious that there was
little time to spare and much to do, I was stirring
early the next morning, despite the fatigue of the
preceding day. It was raining more heavily than
ever; in the dull leaden sky overhead there was no
promise yet of fairer weather. The world of
London read that fact in the dull grey clouds
above its head, and went its course phlegmatically.
There was no lingering in door portals or beneath
shop-blinds that day; business people of position

rodè to their various offices; poorer brethren with much to do walked sturdily on beneath their umbrellas; boys, beggars, and shabby-looking individuals became reckless, and began the day by getting wet through early; the shopkeepers looked disconsolately through their windows—fancy-goods shopkeepers especially.

I was cool and collected at my early breakfast table, at which Mary, ever watchful now, sat facing me. There was a busy day before me; there was much planning and counterplanning to prepare and fight against; in an hour or two at least I should know whether there was a hope of a respite. In the great match between Herbert Vaughan and me, he was master of the game still, and in my heart I had but little hope. It had been a desperate game for months, but he would play it to the end, and care little what he said or did to be the victor in a strife so deadly. There was a fortune to the winner—and if he lost, it might be death to him.

Mary would have accompanied me, had I not begged her to remain at home. I felt still that my interview with her brother would be better without a witness. If that brother stood at bay, he in his bitter malice might strike at her,

whose strength lay only in her love for me. Half
an hour before I started to the —— Hotel to keep
my promise of meeting Herbert Vaughan, Mary
and I talked long and earnestly of what was best
to do and say. After all it was but idle talk, for
there was no guessing what turn the interview
might take, and no preparing against the wiles of
one so specious.

I went away with her whispered adjurations to
be calm—her white face watched me down the
street, and the door closed at last reluctantly.
In that street I met James Baines. Face to
face we came, stared at each other, and passed
on. That man was on the watch for Wenford, and on Wenford's caution must depend the
rest. I could but chance it, and leave it in uncertainty; following James Baines would not avail
me now.

The clocks were striking ten as I reached the
—— Hotel. I ascended the steps, saw the porter
of the preceding night, and sent in my card to Mr.
Vaughan. After a few moments' interim, a
servant appeared to usher me into his presence. I
followed him up a flight of stairs to a room on the
first-floor. He entered and announced me,

" Mr. Gear."

The servant retired, and closed the door upon us.

In a spacious and elegantly furnished room sat Herbert Vaughan—true to the promise which he had made me yesternight. He had risen later than myself, and was seated at a breakfast-table, on which a mass of silver glittered—the *Times* newspaper had been in his hand a moment since, as he lounged on the couch in his handsome dressing-gown.

A gentleman, cool and self-possessed—betraying no excitement at my appearance there.

He rose as I entered, not so much by way of polite attention to myself, as to touch an ormolu bell-handle at the side of the mantel-piece.

"You are punctual to the minute, Mr. Gear," he said shortly and decisively.

"To the minute, sir," I repeated.

"Clear away these things," he said to the servant who responded to his summons; "and admit no one, on any account whatever, until this gentleman withdraws."

"Very well, sir."

The servant departed with the tray, and Mr. Vaughan, abandoning the couch for a damask-covered chair, took his place by the table, leaned his arms thereon, and folded his two white hands complacently together.

"Take a seat."

I did so, and sat down facing him. His keen eyes watched every movement of my own; though he was not alarmed, he was, at least, not uninterested. He made no pretence of treating lightly the nature of the business that had brought us face to face there.

"Now, then," he said, in a low tone.

"I will be brief, Mr. Vaughan. I believe all that I have to say may be conveyed in a very few words."

He nodded his head; there was no reply required to this.

"I will ask if it be your intention to proceed with this trial?"

"It is."

"At all hazards?"

"If there be any—at all hazards."

"I warn you that you have no proofs against that guilt with which you would stain my sister's name."

"I cannot pay any attention to your warnings, sir," he said. "I have no faith in warnings. I map my own course out, and go on to the end, undismayed by the enemies who start up to assail me."

"We shall contest this trial."

"Very well."

"Mr. Wenford will defend himself as co-respondent."

"What gentleman would not, who hoped to raise a shilling upon his honest name?"

"He is in a condition to prove that he left Nettlewood unaccompanied by your wife."

"So am I," he answered, quietly.

"That he went to New York without her—that the woman with the false name, paid to personate my sister, was your tool and accomplice."

"He will have an opportunity of saying all this before the Judge in Ordinary—why come here to put me on my guard against the machinations to defeat my hopes?"

"I come to warn you that you are proceeding to your doom."

"Do I ask you to save me?"

"No."

"Have I warned you to beware of plotting against me in this manner? Surely I have," he asked, more energetically.

"You have warned me once before."

" Once again, then—for the last time!"

"Let me continue—I have not finished yet. To the last farthing of my money shall I employ counsel to represent and defend my sister."

"If the law will allow you!—if it is not too late now!"

"I will be heard, sir," I cried, fiercely; "in the open court, and before heaven, I will denounce you."

"Well—what next?"

"I will brand you as my sister's murderer," I cried; "I will rend to shreds your flimsy veil to hide the truth, which damns you through eternity. I will prove that Ellen was murdered in the Black Gap mountains on the morning of the 21st of July, last year."

He laughed, but his eyes were more intently fixed upon me. There might be an advantage over me in his coolness and self-possession, but I was there to denounce him, and my heart would not beat quietly beneath his insults. That man before me was my sister's murderer, and in his presence there was no calmness for me.

" Murdered in the Black Gap range," I repeated, " by the hand, perhaps, of Janet Muckersie, who crossed the Ferry at your instigation on the night

I mentioned. Ellen fled by the Black Gap range
from the death she feared at your hands, was
followed and foully slain. I will prove her presence there by a ring that was discovered in the
Pass, and which she wore at Mrs. Ray's."

"I prove. this too," was his reply; "Ellen
Vaughan *did* leave my house by means of the
private boat—did proceed by the Black Gap Pass,
as arranged between her and her paramour—was
followed by Janet at my own request, but was
never overtaken."

" And the pistol-shot ?"

" The pistol-shot," he repeated, slowly, "I have
nothing to do with. I shall not be called upon to
explain all the noises that happened on that night
of which you speak."

I saw my scheme to thwart him fading away—
there was but one more arrow left in the shaft. I
sent it flying blindly on its way towards him, and
struck him to the quick.

" And your presence in the Black Gap on that
night when the glove was lost."

His fingers clasped together more rigidly, and
for an instant the colour left his face. But he
kept his eyes upon me still, as though my soul

were bare before him, and he could read all that it expressed.

"You are becoming more vague," he said at last, adding, more scornfully, "*my* presence!"

"Herbert Vaughan—I have that glove."

"You may have fifty if you please."

He had recovered his hard defiant manner—he sat there resolved to brave his way through all, and in my sinking heart I felt how powerless I was.

"It might have been better, perhaps, to have proved collusion in this matter," I said; "to have taken at your word all that you have said to Wenford, and so have dashed your scheme to atoms. But it was more honest to defend her as I will defend her yet, by God's help!"

"Well, I cannot wish you success."

"If my sister live, as you would have me believe, if you know her address, as you would have Wenford believe, give me the proofs, and I will take no further steps in the matter. More, I will beg your pardon for all the evil that I have accused you of."

Herbert Vaughan rose to his full height, and pointed one hand towards me. His eyes were glittering like a serpent's—not brightening with the light of any honest anger.

"Mr. Gear," he said, slowly and calmly, "I have done with you. I defy you—I will even ask you to do your worst against me. My claim to be considered an injured man will be heard in three days time. Appear on that day and tell the judge I am your sister's murderer, and not her scape-goat, if you dare. The world, that is fond of slander, may believe you, perhaps, but the law, which deals with sober facts, will dash down every lie. Mr. Gear, I offered you the hand of friend-ship, and you turned away—then, sir, you lost your chance for ever."

"Not my chance for ever, if God will it," I ex-claimed. "I have begun my search, and will track you to the death! I swear it!"

"You will do your worst," he said; "but I am on my guard, and prepared to meet all invidious attacks. You warn me of danger—but I am pre-pared for it. It steels my nerves and saves my blood from sluggish inactivity. I am proud of my enemy, Mr. Gear."

I could believe that he was the cool, deliberate villain I had ever thought him, to meet his glance then; on his face I could read his whole dark history.

"Mr. Vaughan," I said, struggling to repress that exhibition of passion which had placed me at a disadvantage with him, "I have failed in the object of my coming hither—I have neither deterred you from following up an awful slander, nor affected you by my consciousness of your life's infamy."

"Mr. Gear—I never set myself up for a hero," he replied; "I am aware of all the exaggerated statements which your wife has made concerning me, all the stories on which I might throw a different light if I were disposed to stand upon defence. But I am disposed for nothing save a termination to this interview."

"I have no wish to prolong it."

"Let us part, then," he said, "each strengthened by the purity of his intentions, and buoyed up by the knowledge that God is with the right."

The man's confidence or audacity dismayed me; his calm assumption of superiority over me and my motives even staggered me, who knew so much in his disfavour. My old impression recurred to me that that man played his part well and naturally, for the reason that he submerged himself in his character, and for the time believed that he *was* the injured being, to whom so many evil motives had been attributed.

We were standing facing each other, when the servant knocked at the door.

"Come in," said Vaughan, who was no longer anxious to be undisturbed.

"A telegram, sir. The man is waiting in the hall for an answer, if you please."

"A telegram," he muttered, taking up the sealed envelope from the salver that was presented to him, and turning it over and over in his hand; "very well—tell the man to wait. Good morning, Mr. Gear."

I made a slight movement of the head towards him, and then went slowly across the room towards the door. I was reluctant to leave him; I felt that I had not done my best for Ellen's sake; that I had exposed my plans too much, and failed in beating down the one great scheme which ended with his marriage to Letty Ray. Even then, in the last moments of that interview, I endeavoured to think of some weak point in the armour which encased him, and make one last attempt to touch him; but I had used every effort, and was baffled. I had only proved that Ellen Vaughan had crossed the Ferry on the night of the 21st of July, and he had acknowledged to its truth, and called it part of Ellen's scheme arranged before her flight. I looked back at him when I was in the doorway; the servant had retired to deliver the message, and the open paper was in Herbert Vaughan's hand. He had changed at last! The iron nerve which had resisted all attack of mine was shattered then; the face was ashen, and the hand which held the missive shook like an aspen leaf. He had been struck by the lightning of some truth, to give way so suddenly and utterly as that.

His eyes wandered to where I was standing watching him.

"I thought you were gone," he said, with a composure that I could see was forced at that time; "what are you waiting for?"

"You have nothing to tell me?"

"Nothing."

So we parted. Before I closed the door upon him, I saw him sink into a chair by the table, spread carefully before him the missive which had daunted him in mid-career, and, holding his head between his hands, prepare to study that new mystery.

CHAPTER VIII.

CALLED BACK.

IN the heavy rain I went back home. The wind of the last two days had dropped, but there was no hope of the rain's cessation with it. The banks of cloud which had been drifted onwards by the south-west wind now hung motionless and dense over the city, and shut out all hope of sunshine. It rained more heavily that day than it had done all the week, and I dashed my way through it carelessly. I had become accustomed to this abnormal state of things, and only fine weather would have surprised me much. It was weather congenial to my present mood; my heart was heavy, there was little lightness on the path ahead of me—the path which Ellen had followed, and which ended at the precipice.

I walked home after my usual fashion, and found Mary awaiting my return, feverish with the suspense which had kept her excited and restless during my absence.

"What hope ?" she asked.

"None," was my hollow answer.

We sat down side by side to speak of the interview and the remarks by which it had been characterized. Further action on my side was imperative now; the case at the Divorce Court must be defended, Wenford must be consulted, and forced onward in the cause.

"You will leave the rest to me, Mary," I said; "I am calm and self-restrained, and the way is clear before me. I cannot ask you to be active in a cause that, if successful, will be the ruin of your brother—you will leave the rest in my hands."

"I am thinking of Ellen now," she said boldly; "my sister by marriage—a woman whom he has cruelly oppressed. I will think of him," she added, "when his trouble has come, and he is sorry for all the evil he has caused. Then, Canute," looking timidly into my face, "I will ask you to be merciful to him for your wife's sake."

At this moment the maid-servant entered the room with a letter—*a telegram !*

"Is the man waiting?" I asked.

"Yes, sir."

I tore open the envelope, and my wife hung upon my arm ready to read the first words of the message with me. I felt that there was news of moment beneath my hand—news that would affect all my after-life. The same news which had struck at Herbert Vaughan had come to me.

"Courage, Mary," I said, with a faint smile, "for the worst."

"Or the best, Canute."

I opened the telegraphic missive, which was dated Bowness, and read—

"From Joseph Gear, of Nettlewood Inn, Cumberland, to Canute Gear, of Penton Terrace, New Road, London.

"Come to Nettlewood House at once, by the express, which leaves Euston Square at one P.M. Janet Muckersie will tell all—*must* tell all. Vaughan is on his way hither. I am waiting here at Bowness for an answer from you. I shall expect you at the Ferry Inn to-night. Bring Mary."

"What does it mean?" my wife exclaimed.

"It means that we are close upon the truth, and must go at once."

"Or is it a snare of some one's to take us away from London at this time?"

"I must chance it—I feel that we are nearing the end, Mary."

I sat down to my desk to think of a message to be sent by telegraph to Bowness.

The message perplexed me; after all, it might be a deeply-laid scheme to lure me from London—something on a par with the duplicity that had so long deceived me. What was to hinder a stranger from walking into the telegraph office at Bow-. ness, and forwarding me a missive in my brother's name? What if Janet had departed by a late train last night, reached Bowness, and telegraphed that message to me?—what if Vaughan had been acting to the last? I had fought so long against the elements of surprise, that in everything around me a hidden motive seemed to lurk, and was to be prepared against. How was it possible to elicit the genuineness of this message? An idea seized me at last. I wrote off the following reply—

" I will come down at once. If you are Joseph
Gear, telegraph back immediately to my wife
what you found in the Black Gap Pass on the
morning of the 22nd of July. She waits your
answer."

" I will start at once," I said to Mary, " but the
answer will not reach you by the time to accompany me. If Joseph telegraphs back ' a ring,' come
on by the next train, and I will await you at
Kendal; if there be no reply within three hours,
telegraph to Crewe to me that no answer has been
sent. I shall be at Crewe at seven or eight this
evening, and will proceed at once to the telegraph
office for the message."

I sent off my reply, and then hastened forward
my preparations for departure. I had but little
time before me to reach Euston Square—every
minute was precious—the fever of excitement was
once more upon me, and hurled me forward.
There seemed no hope of rest again.

My arrangements for departure were hurriedly
made, my wife assisting me, and glancing nervously towards me.

When I was prepared to depart, and had once
again run over my instructions to her—what
train she was to take with my mother and child,

what course to adopt, if all were part of a scheme to entrap her—she passed her arms round my neck, and held me to her.

"Oh, Canute!—for my sake, more than ever, you will take care!"

"Trust me."

"If good or evil follow this, I shall still fear the result to you."

"I shall not give way yet a while, Mary—I feel stronger than ever to meet all that may be in store for us at Nettlewood."

A few more last injunctions—a promise from her to leave for Kendal immediately on receipt of a telegram from Joseph Gear—a last embrace—and then I was whirled away in a Hansom-cab to Euston Square. There was little time to spare—only by three minutes did I save the express bound for the north of England.

Half the carriages were already occupied by passengers, who had arrived in better time than myself—late comers were hurrying to and fro in wild bewilderment of purpose—the guards were ready, the engine-drivers were at their posts, the station-master was anxious to be rid of the train.

A miserable day for a long railway-journey; the open road beyond the terminus, misty and grey with the rain still falling—heavily falling from heaven to earth.

I travelled first-class that day—it had not struck me that I had given up my old habit of economy, until the door of the railway-carriage was banged and locked upon me.

There were three occupants of the compartment beside myself—all business men, travelling northwards, with the hope of making money in some way or other, I could see it written on their faces. Stolid and reserved men, whose company suited me just then—who did not want to engage anyone in conversation, but preferred to cross their arms upon their chests, and frown themselves to sleep.

I took my place, and dropped into thought at once; ere the shrill whistle sounded, and the train glided away from the terminus into the density that lay before it, I was thinking of all that lured me from London to the old battle-ground—of all in the past that had gathered round my path, rendered every step doubtful, distracted me, weighed upon my brain, until my confidence in keeping strong began to lessen with my failing strength. I should be ill—I felt that I should be dangerously ill—if the last step led me to another road, on

which no light could fall—I felt that there would
be a morbid happiness in standing at Ellen's grave,
and saying,

"The search is over—here she was hidden by
the guilty hands that snatched her life away!"

A long wearisome journey, despite the rapid progress of the train, the flashing by of station after
station, the dashing along embankments, through
cuttings and tunnels, the difficulty of catching a
glimpse of the landscape through the rain-dotted
glass. My heart beat, and my temples throbbed
unmercifully. I had accustomed myself lately to
long walks, in all weathers, at all times, and this
sitting quietly in a corner of the railway-carriage
strangely irritated me.

We had rattled onwards about an hour, when
one of the business-men, awakened by a more unearthly whistle of the engine than usual, sat blinking at me for a while.

"They're skimming on well now," he said after
a half-grunt by way of preface.

"Do you think so?"

"Don't you?"

"I fancy not—I can't say," was my vague
answer.

The business-man blinked at me again, rubbed

Q 2

at the misty glass, with the palm of a great red hand, then said,

" What a lot of rain we've had lately ! "

" Yes."

" All over the country—my correspondents assure me there is not a town or city in England that has escaped this horrible deluge. Very bad for the farmers, I should say."

" Doubtless, very bad."

" Some of the valleys in Cumberland are flooded, I am told."

" Indeed ! "

I looked up with greater interest.

" What do they say about Nettlewood ? " I asked.

" Where's that ? "

" Beyond the Black Gap range, and near Henlock."

" Don't know anything about that place," he replied; " one of the fancy places for tourists to skulk in, I suppose.   Offers a waterfall, or a mountain, and a chance of breaking one's neck ? A favourite place of yours, perhaps, sir ? "

I shuddered.

" No."

The man curled himself askew, blinked at me

once or twice again, and went off to sleep a second time, to wake no more till the train reached Rugby. It was like a reprieve to dash out of the carriage, and pace the platform like a madman until the few minutes' grace was up, and the train was ready to depart. I lingered till the last moment, and then stepped into the first carriage that was handy to me—without any regard for my old position. I entered a first-class compartment, tenanted but by two persons, both females; here I could remain without a chance of being disturbed by intrusion on my thoughts.

And here my thoughts were intruded upon at the first moment. The lady facing me leaned forward to make sure of the recognition, and then said,

"Mr. Gear—you here?"

"Miss Ray."

"You are going to Nettlewood—you have been sent for suddenly?"

"Yes."

"What does it all mean?" she asked, in almost a beseeching tone; "you who were never an enemy of mine, who was kind to me before I dreamed of riches, and was but a poor waitress at an Inn—you will tell me what it means?"

"Miss Ray, I am in the dark concerning all that may happen in the future. What does Mr. Vaughan say?"

"I have not seen him. I called at his hotel an hour since, and heard that he had started for Cumberland in haste."

"This is no jugglery, then—no plot of Vaughan's."

"It is a mystery," she murmured.

She flung her veil back as if for air. Her companion leaned forward, and asked a question eagerly.

"No," she replied; "I want nothing but peace of mind."

"But you will be calm, Miss Ray—after all, there may be no occasion for alarm."

"There is danger threatening the only one I love in the world," she cried.

"Hush—hush!"

"He knows it," pointing to me; "why should I seek to hide my love for one who will shortly be my husband? Mr. Gear knows all, Miss Carpenter."

"Yes—but——"

"And Mr. Gear will at least tell me, by our past

friendship together, what is taking him to Nettle-wood so suddenly ?"

"Candidly, I have been telegraphed for by my brother."

"Is he ill ?"

"No—but he has been in search for a long while of a truth that has been hidden from me—and I think that he is nearing it."

"This concerns Herbert ?"

"I believe so."

"*He* will strive to affect his honour—to prove him a bad man."

"I am ignorant of all that is waiting for me at my journey's end," I answered.

It was an evasive reply, and she looked eagerly towards me; her face was livid and angular—there was less panic than suspense in her dark eyes—less fear for her future than for the uncertainty of the form it might assume.

"Mr. Gear, I do not think that you are in the plot against my happiness," she said, after a while; "from all that I have known of you, I cannot believe that."

"Miss Ray," I replied, "if any plotting of mine could throw a light upon the mystery of my sister's death, I should have attempted it long since, though your seeming happiness had been blasted by the discovery."

"Why do you call it seeming happiness?"

"We have spoken of this before—surely, at this late hour, I need not give you my opinion of Herbert Vaughan's character."

"Were he a villain, I should be happy with him —my life is bound up with his, for good or evil, now. In all his trouble I stand by him—whatever happens in the future, I will not desert him!"

I could not reason with this excited woman, whose love was a disease—a madness. In her poverty she had brooded upon it till her mind had almost given way: now in her riches she was the same demented girl, who would see no danger on the road Vaughan thought of leading her.

"Miss Ray—pardon me, but I have no sympathy with you. If Herbert Vaughan remains a prosperous man, then I am for ever unhappy—if he marry you, I and those I love are for ever disgraced."

"I know it—I know it," she murmured.

She was silent for awhile; she lay back and closed her eyes—by the light in the carriage-roof above our heads, I thought that she was sleeping. Her companion looked across at me.

"If she were to sleep a little while, it would do her so much good," she said; "a little thing disturbs her now."

"I am not asleep," said Letty, passing one hand across her forehead, "only my head aches, and my brain is on fire. If I only knew the worst, I would face it, and not step back a hair's-breadth."

Another long pause, broken by her impatient snatch at the tassel of a travelling bag her companion carried.

"Where did I put the letter, Miss Carpenter?— the message that was sent to me?"

"In the bosom of your dress, Miss."

"Ah! I had forgotten."

From her dress she drew forth a paper and thrust it into my hands.

"Try and explain that to me—whatever it means."

I opened the paper. It was a telegraphic message, and ran thus:

"From Janet Muckersie, Nettlewood House, Nettlewood, Cumberland, to Miss L. Ray, of Russell Square, London. Herbert Vaughan will

be at Nettlewood House to-night. The Divorce
Case is abandoned for ever. If you wish to hear
the truth, keep strong and come home."

"Abandoned for ever!—thank God!" I ejaculated.

"Thank God for my heart's bitterness—my
shame," she said.

"No, for my sister's fair name, which Herbert
Vaughan had the power to hold up to virtuous
woman's scorn. The power, but not the right!"

"She *was* false to him, Mr. Gear."

"Miss Ray," I replied, firmly, "I will not pain
you by my old assertions—if we are called to hear
the truth, we may afford to be patient until then.
But I—I would warn you to be prepared for a
great shock."

"I am prepared now—I shall be calm soon.
After all, what *is* the worst?"

"God knows."

"It can't dash down my faith in him—it can't
rob me of his love for me—through sin and shame
I follow him to the end. If he dies, I will die
with him."

"Miss Ray—Miss Ray!" pleaded her companion.

"I am quiet now—see how steady my hand is!"

After holding forth her hand, on the left finger of which glittered one single diamond that shone like a fire-speck in the light of the oil-lamp, she wrapped herself in her shawl, and remained silent and moody She closed her eyes again, but they were restless eyes beneath the heavily-fringed lids, and I caught them fixed upon me brightly and steadily, at uncertain intervals. I felt that there were flashes of suspicion which crossed her mind at times, and that she could not shake off the impression that I was connected with the awful truth with which they threatened her. The avowal—often declared—of my want of faith in Vaughan, connected me with the danger which she feared was hanging over him. And yet, strangely enough, her confidence revived at times; I could tell that by her varied mood.

We reached Stafford, where the rain seemed pelting down more violently than ever—it was like the roar of a sea as it fell upon the roof of the station.

"Can I get you any refreshment, Miss Ray?"

"No."

"You look fatigued."

"I am well enough—pray let me be."

Her natural kindness led her to think an in-

stant afterwards of her companion, but Miss
Carpenter also refused any refreshment, at this
stage of the journey. I left the carriage and walked up
and down the platform in the same excited fashion; I
sought no refreshment myself, my heart was sick
with suspense. I returned to the same compartment—there was some satisfaction in accompanying Letty Ray, and watching one who suffered
like myself. It was strange that we two should be
travelling express to the old scene, where both our
wild romances began, and that her feverish excitement should be like my own, for a reason
that was so utterly apart from all my hopes and
fears.

The train whirled away; the darkness of the
night settled down upon us, and the rain, "scurry-
ing" across the open country, dashed against the
carriages like a heavy sea that broke into spray
against the obstacle opposing it.

It was five o'clock when the train clanked its
way beneath the great terminus at Crewe. I
leaped from the carriage, unmindful of my com-
panions, and rushed at the first guard.

"The telegraph office—quick!" I shouted at
him.

"This way, sir."

A civil young fellow, who read the excitement on my face, and felt for it, led the way to the telegraph office, and, waiting not for a fee, dashed back to the duties which the arrival of the express from London had incurred upon him. I entered the office.

"Is there a message left here for Mr. Canute Gear?"

"Yes."

The clerk passed a paper over to me, which I eagerly read.

"*The message was from your brother. I follow by the next train.*"

"When is the next train from London to Kendal?"

"You had better ask the guard. I don't know much about the trains, sir."

But the guards were slamming doors and twisting handles. I dashed at the book-stall, flung down a piece of money for a Bradshaw—to this day I am ignorant of the amount I paid for that wonderful statistical compilation—rushed to the carriage where I had left Miss Ray last.

She and her companion were in their old positions; another traveller had taken up his seat in the corner—another man whom business further north had led to defy the inclemency of the weather.

I set myself to study Bradshaw by the little light afforded by the carriage lamp—to my horror I found that no further train left London for the north that day. The next train stopped at Lancaster, but on referring to other pages I discovered that a train left at three in the morning, reaching Penrith at twenty minutes to five. Would she be informed of this at the station, or discover it by time-tables for herself?—would she come on to Lancaster?

"What disturbs you so much, Mr. Gear?" Letty asked after a while.

There was no occasion to make my motives a secret, and I told her at once.

"My wife promised to follow by the next train, but the only train bound northwards to-night stops at Lancaster—reaching there at midnight."

"Well?"

"And I am uncertain whether she will come by that train, or wait till the next day."

"She must be strangely altered since my past knowledge of her, if she can remain passive till the morning."

" You are right—I will wait for her at Lancaster."

"You love your wife very dearly, Mr. Gear?"

" God bless her!—yes."

" I never thought that you would be happy with her—but I was deceived. Why should *you* not be deceived in judging where my best happiness awaits me?"

Though it was a question, it was directed more to herself thán me. She did not anticipate an answer, but folded herself more tightly in her shawl, and closed her eyes again. She dropped into a half-sleep, half-waking stupor, and soon afterwards started up in her seat with a suppressed cry.

" What a dream!—what a strange dream!"

I did not reply to this, and she leaned across and said, in as low a tone as the clatter of the train would permit,

"I thought I was at the lake again, and you had your arms round me drawing me from the water. Oh, sir!—was it for the best?"

" Surely, Letty, for the best."

" You prophesied about the brightness of my future, then. This *is* the future you were thinking of at that time!"

"No, Letty — further away still — further away."

"If all that you believe could become my belief too, I could curse you for that rescue now."

She lay back, and held up her hand, when I would have replied to her.

She closed her eyes, and once I heard her moan forth,

"Oh! this dreadful never-ending journey!"

The time dragged on, despite the rain and rush of the train; hour after hour shut in by the same thoughts of danger and uncertainty—conscious of being borne towards the truth—whatever it might mean, or whose whole after-lives it might affect. Throughout that long journey Letty refused all refreshment, and her companion thought her example worthy of imitation, although she made a few furtive nibbles at some biscuits stored at the bottom of her travelling-bag.

Close upon nine o'clock, when the train reached Lancaster at last—Lancaster, where the everlasting rain had followed us.

"You stay here," Letty asked.

"Yes—I am compelled."

"I shall be at Nettlewood by daybreak—I post all night."

" I shall follow you as soon as possible."

" I will warn him that you are on your way towards him, sir," she said, with her old suspicion. " If you bring evil with you, he must guard against it."

"Tell him I am coming, if you will," I answered. " My arrival is no secret."

I had stepped from the carriage ; she had lowered the window, and sat there looking out, with the rain beating against her face. I bade her good night, but she motioned me to stay an instant. In that last moment there came upon her an awful fear of danger to her lover—perhaps of his unworthiness, despite her woman's faith, which clung to him through all !

" Mr. Gear," she whispered suddenly, " if the power be in your hands at the last, you will be merciful?"

" Miss Ray—I will be just."

" But if——" her face flushed, she turned away to draw up the window with an impatient clang, and shut me and her passing fear away from her. The shrill whistle rang into the night again—the train moved on, and left me standing there, with a few passengers damp and shivering like myself.

"Guard, how much more rain are we going to have?" asked a facetious traveller of the man who stood under the lamps examining the tickets.

"Not much more, I hope, sir. Thank you, sir."

"Much damage done about here?"

"Heaps, sir."

"Ah! we haven't seen the end of it yet. Good night."

"Good night to you, sir."

CHAPTER IX.

THE LAST STAGE.

WEARISOME yet feverish hours of expectancy between the departure of the last train and the arrival of the next, in which I hoped to find my wife. The station after a while deserted; the little waiting-room with the fire left to burn out, and the coal-scuttle removed for fear of depredations on my part; some one behind the partition where the tickets were given out occupied for a while in counting money, and scratching with a very bad pen; finally relapsing into slumber and snoring in a disjointed manner, that told of troubled dreams.

I walked up and down the deserted waiting-

R 2

room, too restless to attempt to sleep; too anxious
to leave the station and make a dash through the
rain for an hotel; too excited to sit still and take
my strange position quietly. Occasionally, when
the scene became too wearisome, and the ticking
of the clock too unbearable, I made a dash for the
platform, and took a survey of the long sweep of
iron road, the dark landscape around it, the
dots of light from the signal lamps, the signal
house, where a cheerful fire was burning, and
where the figure of a man passed before the
brightness now and then. Occasionally some
little signs of activity woke up the place for a
while; a luggage train heavily laden would rush
by; a guard would emerge from some mysterious
quarter, and look sleepily after it; the colours of
the signal lights would change perhaps; the train
would recede; the red lamps behind the last truck
fade away in the darkness; the guard disappear;
the signal lights be once more expressive of a clear
field ahead and no danger; and then the noisy
rattle of the never-ending rain.

I felt no bodily fatigue—I was only heart-sick
with impatience to be once more moving onwards.
Sometimes I accused myself of want of interest in
Ellen's fate, in the retribution which was coming

to him who had so ruthlessly scathed my sister's
happiness, that led me to halt midway upon my journey, and await Mary's arrival. In the hours I lost
by this inaction, what might not be lost in the distant country whither Vaughan and Letty Ray
had already sped? Then I thought of my delicate
sensitive wife reaching Lancaster in the dead of
night without a friend to assist her, reaching
there in the hope of finding me, and meeting but
strangers' faces glowering at her loneliness.

At half-past eleven o'clock, signs of life at
Lancaster became apparent once more; two guards
made their reappearance; the snoring behind the
ticket partition ceased; some one in the distance
ran backwards and forwards in the rain, swinging
a lantern to and fro, and representing business at
least. Twelve o'clock struck, and no signs of the
train; the guards, perfectly unconcerned about the
delay, and inclined to smile at my questions respecting its non-arrival, one of them sitting on
the edge of a barrow and counting some loose
coppers which he had drawn from his trousers'
pocket. Finally, to my relief the whistle heard
ringing out in the distance, then the fiery eyes of
the engine looming forth and coming nearer and
nearer to the station. The train at its journey's

end at last, and the travellers leaping from the
train to the platform, and staring around them in
rather a scared manner, after the fashion of travellers in general. Last and best of all—my wife,
looking from the window of a first-class carriage,
in search of the one friendly face for which she
had sacrificed so much.

"Mary!"

"Canute!" she cried, "oh! I am so glad that
you are here!—although I scarcely expected—
scarcely hoped—to see you. I thought you would
have proceeded to Penrith by the train, and left
your mother, baby and me, to follow you."

"No, together in this—however it may end."

I assisted my wife and mother to alight—my
mother, who held her grand-daughter in her arms,
and would not part with her on any account.
Outside the station a fly was waiting, in the hope
of a chance customer. This I secured, and placed
them within, returning once more to the office to
rap at the partition behind which the clerk was
still ensconced. The ticket-hole was opened, and
the sleepy eyes of a clerk regarded me.

"What do you want?"

"Is there a possibility of telegraphing to Penrith to-night?"

"Not the slightest—the telegraph clerk has left."

"Can he be found ?"

"If he could, we couldn't find the clerk at Penrith; the office is closed and locked there by this time."

"Thank you."

Resigning this attempt, I returned to the fly, and was giving the man orders to drive to the nearest hotel, when a railway guard touched me on the shoulder.

"Beg pardon, sir, but do you wish any message to be left at Penrith ?"

"Yes—how can it be done ?"

"There's a luggage train will stop just by at half-past one—it's going on to Penrith—I daresay Bill won't mind leaving any message for you at the station, sir."

"I want a post-chaise to meet the train that reaches Penrith at twenty minutes to five. At any expense—if it can only be ready for me."

"Post-chaise !—where to, sir ?"

"Nettlewood."

"Through Keswick and Borrowdale ?"

"Yes—that route."

"Bill can find some one to see after it. Bill's going on to Edinbro' himself."

"Well, I will leave it to you and Bill. Share this with him."

I placed a half-sovereign in the man's hand, together with my card, to be left at Penrith, and then entered the fly.

"Have you both courage and strength to start again in three hours?" I asked of my wife and mother.

"To start anywhere with you," answered Mary. "I have long since forgotten my old sensitiveness to cold—or rather that old sensitiveness which my brother persuaded me into."

"Ah! he was plotting then against my happiness—he did not wish that we should meet too often," I murmured.

"Still he did not thwart *that* happiness, at least," said Mary. "Oh! Canute," in a lower tone, inaudible to my mother, "you will be merciful to him—my only brother—if the power be left in your hands?"

"When we know all, and I possess that power, I will think of you, Mary."

"You are more than generous."

I made an effort to turn the subject, and with some difficulty succeeded. Until the power was in my hands to check his present villainy, it was but idle talking. Generous or just, it was never my intention to leave that man wholly free to work his schemes elsewhere; had he been my own brother, in lieu of Mary's, I should have exacted some stern reparation. And what reparation was sufficient for all that he had done to me and mine?—for all the evil he had plotted against our lasting peace?

At an hotel, where I made some little attempt to eat and drink, with but small success—where Mary came to my side again, and bade me keep strong and hopeful yet.

"Hopeful!" I exclaimed.

"Hopeful of the better days in store for us, when those shadows belong to the past—when we have shown to Herbert, to Janet, that we are not merciless avengers."

"Do not plead for them again. If it be possible, let us forget them for awhile."

The hours were long before it was time to return to the station; until all was ended for good or evil, I knew now there was no peace for me. I could not take peace to my side, and wait patiently the coming of events—even my wife's presence was but little comfort, I thought, now the anxiety concerning it had abated. Was it

possible that I should ever know peace of mind
again ?   When the grim end came, and I was
face to face with it, would not the result for ever
keep me aloof from the happiness that I had known
once ?

My mother spoke little during the whole
journey ; it was all very unreal and dream-like to
her.   No one had offered her an explanation ; and
she had not asked for one.   She knew that Ellen's
name, and that our interest in Ellen was taking us
back to Nettlewood, and she had been advised by
Mary not to harass me with questions which it
would be impossible to answer yet awhile.

If the truth were coming towards us, the time
for explanation would be soon enough for this poor
mother, who believed not in Ellen's death.

We started for the station at ten minutes to
three—at three o'clock, we were once more waiting
in the rain for the arrival of the down train.   At
a few minutes past three, we were once more whirl-
ing onwards—following in the track of her who
had vowed to love him to the last.   On through
the darkness, at a swift rate along the iron road—
thank Heaven, once more in action !   One stop-
page at Kendal, and then dashing forward fiercely,
at a rate that stirred my blood at last—fiercely

and madly to the end in view, through the darkness of the night, to the light wherein all mystery was to die!

We reached Penrith at twenty-five minutes to five—five minutes before time. Of a guard, who was waiting on the platform, I asked if a post-chaise had been procured for Mr. Gear and family.

"Yes, sir; the waiter of the hotel did not like to chance it at first, but remembered you as Mr. Sanderson's partner, and it's been waiting these five minutes."

"Thank God!"

We passed from the platform, through the station, to the post-chaise.

"How long a time to reach Nettlewood?"

"Four hours and a half, or five hours, if we're not kept long at the posting-houses, sir."

"That will be ten o'clock when we reach Nettlewood."

"Thereabouts, sir."

"A sovereign a piece extra if we are there before ten."

"We'll do it, sir."

We were dashing by the main road to Keswick a few minutes afterwards; in a little while

it would be like home again amongst the hills—
had the sun risen, and the rain and mist been less
heavy in those regions, the sight of the mountains
in the background would have soon reminded us
of the cottage at Borrowdale, where, at least, were
only fair reminiscences.

"When shall we settle down again peacefully,
Canute?" asked my wife, clasping her hands upon
my arm, as she sat by my side.

"Presently—presently!"

"You will not give way?—you have promised
me!"

"Strong to the end—if, when the end comes,
I am a little weary, I shall have a faithful
nurse."

"Canute," she said, fearfully, "you feel ill?
The excitement has been too much for you."

"I hope not. I am a little fatigued with the
long journey—presently—presently, Mary, we
shall all be well and happy again. What is to-
morrow?"

"The eighteenth of November."

"Two days before the divorce case. If Vaughan
should not be at Nettlewood, after all!—should
be now hurrying back to strike his last
blow!"

"Patience, Canute—you that have been ever patient. Mr. Wenford remains in London to defend his case."

"Ah! I had forgotten him—we may rely upon him?"

"Yes; I have seen him—he knows now how much he has been deceived."

"He will——"

A soft white hand was pressed upon my lips.

"Try and sleep—pray, do not speak any more of this just now."

I was silent; I lay back and closed my eyes to set her mind at rest, but I might as easily have flown to Nettlewood as slept at that time.

We clattered along the road; the morning was as dark and dense as the night; no sign of daybreak was yet visible; nothing was stirring on the way; the silence of death would have dwelt upon that desolate track, had not the echoes been aroused by our hurried progress through the country, and the hiss, hiss! of the steadily descending rain. Daybreak at last, and the faint gleam of dawn lighting up our pale faces in the carriage.

"You have been sleeping, dear!" said my wife with some exultation.

"It will do me good," I replied, evasively.

"Are we nearing Keswick?"

"Not yet, I think—but the mists are very heavy here."

"We are nearing the mountain land," said my wife. "If the sky were clear we should see dear old Skiddaw once more."

"You speak of the mountains now, as though you loved them, Mary?"

"I have been unhappy in London—in London your strength has been failing—you were brighter, happier here."

"Dear old Skiddaw, then—under its shadow we spent our quiet honeymoon."

"And little Ellen was born in our mountain home—the Ellen that has come, like a blessing, to replace the old."

"Ah! if the old Ellen had died quietly in her youth and beauty—died even of a broken heart —I might have thought so."

The day became lighter—the landscape took its colours from the daybreak—through the rain we could see the fields and hedgerows of the valley, and the base of the mountains, whose tops were hidden in the mist. After a while we were dashing into Keswick, and those townsfolk who had risen betimes, stood about the paved street watching the cortége.

A change of post-horses was procured here; those of the neighbours who recognized me, came forward to welcome me home, and kindly undertook a message for Mr. Sanderson, who would be stirring in the town presently; an early breakfast, or rather the ceremony of one, was gone through whilst the horses were being changed, and then we were off again, dashing away from the fair Lake of Derwentwater, and the broad road that left Borrowdale and home behind us, through Portinscale and Braithwaite, keeping on our left, in the disance, the great mountain range, across which cut the Black Gap Pass, steeped in impenetrable cloud that morning. Hour after hour passing by, the horses changed once more, the last stage of the journey began, coming near well-known scenes, approaching, at last to Henlock, over Henlock Bridge, and then madly, furiously, to keep up a character for speed, and earn the sovereigns handsomely, dashing down the Vale to Nettlewood.

"Half-past nine, sir!" cried the nearest postboy, as I looked out of the carriage-window.

" Well done ! "

" There's the Ferry, sir—and here's some one running towards us, I think."

It was Joseph, who, at a rate of progression very remarkable for him, came towards the post-chaise.

" Stop ! "

The carriage stopped when we were facing Joseph. He opened the door, and clambered into the post-chaise.

"Don't go to the Ferry Inn," he gasped; " that would lose time, and we're wanted further on."

"; At Nettlewood House ? "

" No—at Miss Ray's. To face Vaughan at last with all the proofs we have gathered together."

" He is there, then ? "

" Yes ; and anxious to hear the worst. If he tried to escape, it would be of no avail—I think he only hopes for mercy now. Miss Ray is very anxious to see you. Well, mother ? "

" Well, my dear son—what—what of Ellen ? "

" You will know all directly. I have promised to say nothing. Canute," he said, suddenly lean-ing forward, " you owe me eight and sixpence for

that last telegram to Mrs. Gear—it's of no con-
sequence just now, but of course it was at your
own expense."

CHAPTER X.

IN THE NET.

THE post-chaise drove us direct to Miss Ray's
mansion—the house which I had first planned in
the matter-of-fact life preceding this—which had
caused all the varied changes that had come upon
us all.   Had the advertisement in the *Builder*
newspaper never crossed me, or I had failed to be
successful, what a different end to this story!
When I crossed the ferry at Nettlewood, if I had
dreamed of all the changes that my presence
would effect, and of all the crime which evolved
therefrom, I should have turned back on my way,
and have never met with Mary Zitman.

And yet, that one stop backward would have

been shutting from light and life the wife who had found happiness with me—dooming her ever to solitude and want of sympathy. Her happiness and mine for ever lost—but Ellen by my side, unknowing the dangers to which she had approached so closely. All so different even—the lady of the mansion to which we were approaching, still the dark-browed and sullen maiden of the Ferry Inn, surely a better life for her, a fairer than the future one in store. I had attained happiness by the step that brought me to Cumberland—happiness so far as it related to my own home and household gods—but I had brought danger and death to others, and evil had followed like a shadow on my track. Yes, better to have turned back, I thought, and known nothing of the troubled hearts that beat in that green-vale!

The post-chaise dismissed—the heavy demand upon my purse met—we went along the carriage-drive together.

On the threshold of Miss Ray's house, a woman without a bonnet, but thickly hooded, met us.

"I ha' been waitin' for ye all."

"Janet!" I exclaimed.

"Ay, Janet!" she replied, "ye need na' luke

sae scared. I hae been waitin' this day, which she would ha' forestalled—the day o' my shame and her humiliation."

"Will there be no more mystery?—no more to perplex us after this, Janet?" my wife asked.

"Na mair—a' noon-dayglare, cruel and sarchin' eno' to maist o' us."

She turned to my mother and touched her shawl.

"Ye are auld, and a shock such as be coomin'— a story sic as I hae to tell—is na gude for ye. Will ye tak the bairn up-stairs to a room which the servant will shew ye, and let yer son tell the story afterwards? It will be sae muckle the better for ye, ma'am."

"Canute?"

My mother turned to me as if for advice.

"So much the better, mother," I repeated.

"Well—I will go, then."

Janet turned to the maid-servant, and whispered a few words in her ear; the servant nodded, and then asked my mother to follow her.

"The rest can follow me. Ye can stap awa' if ye like," turning on Joseph somewhat suddenly.

"Thank you, but I prefer to accompany the rest."

"Wull, ye hae a right, mayhap—do as ye list."

Janet led the way along the hall, more like the mistress of the house than the servant—at the library door she paused, holding the handle very firmly for awhile.

"I'm na sae strang as I used to be, and this be a sair trial to a woman who ha' leeved sae lang in hope o' *him*."

The shawl dropped from her head, and her dishevelled grey hair, fell about her face. She pushed the hair back behind her ears, and looked a little wildly at us.

"We ha' roon doon—ye need na be too hard, now your day's coom to triumph."

"A sad triumph, Janet," I remarked.

"Ay!—who kens that sae weel as I?"

She turned the handle of the door, and entered, saying,

"They've coom!"

We followed, and a man at the end of the table, who had been seated there with a book before him, looked up at us in a strangely nervous manner—a manner very strange for him—and then looked down again. It was Herbert Vaughan, the man who by some chance, to me wild and inexplicable, was brought to bay at last!

I looked round for Miss Ray, but she was not present yet.

"Miss Ray will na be here a weel," said Janet, calmly.

"Why not?" was Vaughan's answer.

"She ha' not the strength—all this ha' been a shock to her."

"Well—well!"

Vaughan idled with the leaves of the book he had feigned to be interested in; then he looked up again with that strange anxiety or nervous suspense which I had before remarked.

"I am in your hands, sirs," he said, addressing my brother and myself; "I am here at your bidding. You have tracked me to the death, but you have promised to be merciful. Let us arrange all together quietly, and spare the world a confession that can do no good. What is required of me?—and who is my accuser?"

There was a long pause; I looked towards my brother, but he sat very still, with his thin hands clasped together.

"You must remember that I am strangely in the dark as yet," he said; "that a message from my housekeeper, Janet, has brought me hither to meet you. She tells me that everything is known by you, and that my safety only lies in coming hither. That away is danger, but here may be forgiveness. I am prepared for the worst. Who flings the first stone at me ?"

He looked up with a glance of his old defiance ; then his features changed, and his face assumed a deadly whiteness, as Janet suddenly rose and stood at the end of the table facing him.

" I DO !" she answered.

" You—you ?"

He clutched the table with both hands, and glared at Janet as though she were a spirit. Whatever he believed was known, whatever calamity he had prepared for, he did not think of this faithful servant of his house becoming his accuser. It was the first blow aimed at him, and it told. It brought twenty years more to his looks on the instant.

" I see all now !" he gasped.

" I am yer accuser, Herbert Vaughan," she said; " God kens how muckle raither I would ha' laid doon and deed than seen this awfu' day. I saw it coomin' lang since. I kenned that it wad happen at this time—it war a' thocht o' afore yer cunnin'," turning to my brother, " caught at part o' the truth, and would ha' branged aboot my ruin."

"I beg your pardon, Janet," said Joseph, humbly.

"Not ye, or the likes o' ye, that mak me turn agin him at the last," said Janet; "but himsel'— his ain sel' that tuke no warnin', but went on, on in his cruelty, until he faced the truth. Oh! maester," turning to him with a touching earnestness, "if ye had ony been sorry for a' the evil ye ha' been the cause on, if ye had ony gi'en ane sign that ye war na a' eevil, I wad hae been wi' ye in this trial noo."

"Traitress!" he muttered.

"Na that," cried Janet, firing at the word, and drawing herself up proudly; "na that, e'en noo. Had I been a traitress, ye micht ha' deed years ago upo' a gallows; but I held my peace, and watched ower ye, and did my best to sav' yer wilfu' sool. Ye war greedy for goold, and luved it beyon' human life—and when I dooted ye first, wi' *her* first husband," pointing to my wife, "I kep' my watch upo' ye for your ain sak'. They war ony doots, and I would na ha' them certainties, or try to mak them sae. But when it cam to choose atween the auld nurse's luve for ye, and for yer sister Mary—when ye turned agin her, and sought to stap her happiness in ilka wa', I gav ye up at ance. I luved her best o' a', and I *did* strive for her happiness at least."

"My dear Janet!" cried Mary.

"Bide awa, we are na' gettin' to the end yet awheel. When I chose atween him and ye on ye're bridal day, Mary Gear, it war na that I luved him maist, but that I kenned I could serve ye and yeers muckle better by my stay here. I believed e'en then that I saw danger to his puir young wife, and I stayed to watch ower her, and be her help, if need war. And the need came."

She pushed the grey hair back behind her ears again, and struggled with her breath. I leaned forwards with eager interest for her next words; my wife, as if fearful of me still, clasped her hands upon my arm. Vaughan turned his face away from us, and looked fixedly at the opposite wall, a man powerless to act.

"I saw the danger theecken round the braw wife, but she did na luve me, and believed me her husband's spy; I cudna undeceive her wi'oot betrayin' mysel' to him, and I warked on in my ain wa', and kep my watch. She lo'ed that mon--her ane unhappiness war to see how soon his passion passed awa' frae her, when he war left a puir mon by his sister's marriage. Then the temptation cam to him to try for the money in anither fashion—and then I kenned that the wife's life war in mortal danger. I watched on then—I heerd the lees he told his wife aboot Wenford bein' his creditor to a large amoont, and how necessary it war to pay him coort, and humour him. That war the first step—what the ithers war I need na say, but step by step, to murder he went on, thinking not o' the watch I kep for that puir girl's sak'. She guessed half o' the truth at last —mayhap mair than half—and becam gallied aboot her future, jealous, as war natural eno', aboot Miss Ray, to whom that mon spak false aboot his wife, pavin' the wa for the last blow. Well, the blow cam at last, and I war waitin' for it. Ye remember the nicht o' the ball that tuk place in this hoose?"

"Well," I gasped, "go on."

Vaughan rose, and turned his white face towards us.

"Why need I stop here?—why am I compelled to hear this story? Let me go home—I promise you that I will wait you there."

"Ye ha' better stap, sir," said Janet, earnestly ; "there is muckle to do yet—yer signature is re-

quired to ane or twa documents—ye ha' a promees
or twa to mak afore ye leave *us*."

"I am a prisoner," he said, sitting down again.

"I am here to speer far mercy far ye."

"You ?—a murderess !"

Janet struggled with her breath at this retort;
the effect produced by it appeared to restore Vaughan somewhat to himself, to suggest perhaps a
loophole for escape.

"All that this woman has to say is beyond
confirmation," he said; "she makes a charge
against me, to screen herself—mark that !"

"I will mak' the charge at least—these here
wull listen to yer defence, and judge atween the
twa. Ye hae forgotten somethin', Mr. Vaughan
—a forged letter, for instance."

He did not answer. The flash of spirit had
died out, or the gleam of hope that, for a moment,
had deceived him, was shut away from his darkened life again.

"The ball tuke place, and afore that ball—twa
hoors afore—my maister and his wife talked lang
and secretly thegither. He tald her then that he
war a ruined mon, and must fly the country—he
confessed to haein' forged Wenford's name, which

war na true—and o' the necessity that existed for
them baith to become the best o' freends to him,
as he at least war wholly in Wenford's power.
Then he told her that they must baith secretly
leave Nettlewood thegether, and when ance in
safety ask Maister Wenford's mercy. He tald
her that the marning war too late, that a' would
be foond oot, and that by some means unguessed
at, they mun be in a place o' safety befair daylicht.
His wife dooted a' this, but he hae the gift of
arnestness, and she war at last conveenced—or half-
conveenced. Howe'er muckle she dooted him, she
did na believe that he envied her her leef. That
nicht, after the ball, Herbert and his wife crassed
the lake by the private boat, and ganged by the
Black Gap Pass to Borrowdale. Fearing that the
end war coomin', and that life war at stake, I
creepit oot o' the hoose, and made for the ferry-
boat, with which I crassed lower doon the lake.
They war some distance befair me, and. I toiled
hard to gain upo' them, and hear their footsteps in
the Gap—to pray, as I ne'er prayed afore or sance
—that I had meesjudged him, and that he ha' not
murder in his thochts. Then—then the scream of
ane in distress cam', and I felt that I war too late
to be o' help at last. I ran on, prayin' to my

God for help—I cud do naethin' else—the scream
war half a mile awa', doon the descent o' the Gap
into Engerdale. When I reached the tap, the
moon bruk oot, and lit oop the mountain side—half
wa doon I saw the feegure of a woman who had
got awa' frae the grip o' her murderer, fleein'
doon the path pursued by—*him!*"

" A lie !" cried Vaughan.

" I swar to this—mair, I swar to the woman
wha kenned the path better than he, gaining
groond, and the pistol which I had held in my
hand, to fire at him, if it were necessary, I put
back in my pocket. At the same instant, he
fired at her, and she fell face forwards doon the
cliff! The moon went in again, and a' war dim
and dark, as I groped my wa' towards the murderer and his victim. I foond them—I cam' upon
them like a speerit—he war bending over her,
lying sae silent at his feet."

" Go on," I whispered, eagerly.

" He war sair scared at my presence there—he
went doon upo' his knees afore me, and begged me
to keep his secret, told me how he had been
tempted on to this—how false she had been to him
since her marriage. With blude upo' his hands—
the moon came oot again, and I saw it there, dark

and shinin'—he stood and leed his wa' to an excuse for the awfu' deed committed ; he tald me o'
my auld luve for him, our lang connection, and
how it war in my ain hands to save his life or
hang him. And I sided wi' him, and agreed to
help him to bury his wife in the sheep-fold lying
oot o' the track at the head of Engerdale Vale. I
sided wi' him for my leef's sak', I sided wi' him
for the sak' of the victim we carried doon the
steep thegither—fording the river, and passing on
to the ruined sheep-fold, where a' war awfu' darkness. Then we talked thegither, and he, whose narves
had been strung to do this deed, gave wa' and war
anxious to be gane. He sat doon on the rock, that had
fallen through the roof, and sat and sheevered wi'
his face awa' frae her upo' the groond—he owned
at last that he could do nae mair to help me. I
kenned that part of this war actin', to mak' me
his accomplice, or put, at some future day, the
bluidy deed upo' me—but the fear, or the acting,
I thanked my God for then. I war anxious to be
alane wi' the body, and I toold him that if he
would leave it to me, I had the strength to bury it.
I war a po'erful woman, and I war aware o' a
quarryman's shed half a mile doon the Vale, where
tools war kep that wad be o' service to me ; I

took it a' upo' my ain hands, and he thanked me, promeesed me gowld for my services, and hurried awa' doon the Vale, where we found the shed, and tuke frae it a spade and pick. Then he left me, he thanking me for a' my services, and promeesing to wait for me to tak' me hame in his boat—which he did—I to hasten back to the sheep-fold where I left the body."

"Janet, you are guilty by your own confession," said Vaughan, his face lighting up again; "you have been tracked by Joseph Gear, and would now implicate me in a crime which you cannot shake off by any means in your power. I have heard all—now hear my story."

"Ane moment mair," said Janet, quickly; "I hae na doon yet—whilst you hae been schemin' to elude me, my proofs hae been getting awfu' strang. At eleven o' the clock, there wull be a witness on the auld nurse's side."

A time-piece, in a black marble case, struck eleven as she spoke, and instinctively we all turned towards the door, which opened as we looked. Three women entered, one of whom came swiftly towards me, and flung her arms round my neck, as I started up with a wild cry.

"NELLIE!"

" —The witness in her own defence—who has been biding her time, and gaining strength for this day. Herbert Vaughan, do you believe in one risen from the dead?"

He buried his face in his arms and fell forwards on the library table, hiding his looks of horror and guilt from all of us.   He gave up then for ever!

CHAPTER XI.

SPELL-BOUND.

"Not dead! Living and breathing in the midst of us, and giving hope of better days in store for all. Oh! Ellen, I did not dream of such a happy termination to this mystery."

"Not you, 'Patience Gear'!"

"I had long since outlived all patience at your own hard fate. So cruel and undeserved as it seemed!"

"You are here to make the fate less stern for me—to take my part against that man?"

"If it be necessary—you do not fear him now?"

"No."

Her arms relaxed their hold, she stooped and kissed my wife, and then went on to Janet's side and laid her hand upon her arm.

" Faithful friend, whom in the past I misjudged so much, and to whom I owe my life—let me finish the story which in its relation has tried you so acutely."

"I hae tuld them a'—the rest be easy to guess at."

" No one can guess at all your love and faithful service. A few words, and then to other matters, Janet."

Janet sat down, leaned her forehead on her hand and groaned. All this had been a trial to her indeed. Of her own free will she had struck at the idol she had loved so long.

" My husband shot me in the shoulder, but I feigned death, and in his excitement he was deceived. When Janet appeared I gave all up for lost, for she, bending over me, discovered that I lived. My heart leaped for joy when I felt the pressure of her hand—the reassuring hope that I was with a friend. They carried me to the sheep-fold, where they left me, Janet finding an opportunity to whisper ' Courage !' When she returned I had succeeded in stanching the blood,

although the wound continued very painful.
Janet bandaged it for me, and assisted me down
the Vale, intending to stop at the first quarryman's
cottage we could find—but long before the day
broke, we met with a man proceeding with his
cart towards the Pass beyond the Gap, and which
led on to the quarry. The man was a stranger to
Engerdale, and knew us not—for a sum of money
he agreed to drive me to the foot of the Vale,
where the stage coach passes early in the afternoon. Here I parted with Janet for awhile, en-
joining her to secrecy, and promising to remain
silent as the grave concerning all the horrors of
that night. It was arranged between us that
Vaughan was to believe me dead, and I, still in
the dark concerning the purpose that could have
led him to attempt my life, resolved to keep silence
until his future acts betrayed him—and it was
time to thwart his further plotting. I went
to London, where I remained hidden—where
I was supported by money sent by Janet,
whence I watched the progress of the Divorce
Case, and bided my time to baffle him—where
I gathered strength slowly to defend myself.
For some months I lay ill of my wound, nursed by
strangers, even looked upon with suspicion by

them, encouraged only by Janet, writing to me
now and then—begging me to remain concealed a
little longer for her master's sake, who would repent some day—she was sure he would, she wrote!
There, in the last few days, Janet joined me,
hopeless of her master now, and told me the
story of how she had begged him on her knees to
give up his purposed marriage—to relinquish his
design of obtaining a divorce. She gave him up
at last, and sided with me wholly. It was at my
request that Janet came to your apartments in
the New Road, Canute—I had heard of your
mental excitement, and the effect that it was having on you. To discover myself then, I feared
might prove dangerous to you—therefore it was
Janet's intention to break the truth to your wife,
when you arrived to thwart her. I had gone back
to Nettlewood then, to end all—to bring that man
back from London to face the evil he had conjured up around him—and Janet's ill-success was
not known to me until I learned it from her own
lips here in Nettlewood. Then it was too late,
there was no time to spare, and Joseph, who had
followed on a false track concerning Janet, had to
be taken into our confidence and consulted as to
this step."

A long silence followed this explanation. Vaughan retained his inflexible position ; we sat grouped at the further end of the table, my mother stood at the back of us ; whilst close against the door, watchful of all, and looking strangely mournful at all before her, stood Letty Ray, the woman who had vowed to love him to the last. Outside, beyond the large bow-window that gave light to the room, we could see the hurrying glancing rain, the background of leaden sky, growing more dense and dark with every instant—a day befitting the terrible story of man's cupidity and baseness.

"Herbert Vaughan, do you wish to ask a question of me ?"

"No," he murmured.

"Do you expect mercy from me?—your injured wife—the woman who loved you with all a girl's passionate attachment, until the villain followed the lover whom you feigned so well ?"

He did not answer.

"Herbert Vaughan, you will go your way in life, and leave me to my desolate freedom—you will go your way, punished by your own conscience —you will quit England for ever."

"I do not understand," he said, leaning back in his chair, and looking askance at her.

"A deed of separation has been drawn up by my solicitors—you have to sign it; you have therein to sign to my innocence, and your own duplicity—and then God make you a better man, and not give you up as I do."

"And after that?"

"You will leave England—it is my wish; the only condition to my forgiveness of your treachery towards me. Canute," turning to me, "you will not thwart me in these intentions—it is my promise to Janet—it is my own desire that this man should have time before him to repent."

"He will never repent!"

"Still—let him go. It is not justice; but oh! brother, it is forgiveness—a woman's forgiveness for all his evil conduct."

"Ellen—in your heart rests there any of the old love—the old strange fascination that was akin to magic—for that villain there?"

"Nothing but horror of him."

"Let him go, then—let him vanish away to the darkness, now and for ever."

"Where is the deed?" he asked.

Ellen produced it; he ran his eyes hurriedly over it, then signed it, and rose with steps that tottered very much.

"I—I will go now. I must have air."

"Alone on your journey for ever—alone with the consciousness of evil—try to pray for a new heart and better life," said Ellen.

"Na, not alane," said Janet, moving towards him; "if he wull begin life a deeferent mon, and trust in me to be faithful to him still. Mr. Vaughan, will ye think that I did a' for the best, and tried hard to save your sool? Will ye let me dee in serving ye, and be the ane servant true to ye, where'er ye may gang? I will ha' hope and faith in ye again—the wee bairn I nursed in your puir mither's time."

"I will go my way alone—I am tired of spies! I am sick of life!"

He walked on with the same tottering steps to the door, putting a hand forward to keep his sister back, who would have sprung to him to assure him also of her own forgiveness. Further still, at the door itself, where the woman he had hoped to marry was standing watching all this, grave and stern.

"All this for your sake," he said, passing out.

She made no movement to stop him ; she stepped aside, and stood with her hands clasped rigidly together, long after his feet had ceased to echo along

the marble passage, after the door had closed
heavily behind him, and he had gone on in the rain
and mist to his solitary home, a home even deserted by the servants, to whom he had sent down
orders to leave the week preceding—the week
wherein he had been exultant and successful.

Ellen was standing near Janet, leaning over her,
and endeavouring to console her, when Mary quitted
my side to add also her consolation to one who sat
there bowed down by the trials of that day. I
turned to Miss Ray, who did not look up as I approached her.

"Letty, all this has happened for the best."

"They say so," was the bitter answer.

"Surely you do not feel aggrieved at the turn
affairs have taken?   It is rather your place to thank
God for your escape."

"I am glad that I have been all my life mistaken
in your sister—I am sorry that I have no excuse
to offer for my own folly—I acknowledge that
all that has happened he has deserved, and that
you have been more than merciful—but I am not
thankful for all this."

"Why not?"

"It is the beginning of my misery—for ever

after this, a desolate and benighted life for me ! "

"This is morbid folly. Any girl of honest principle would feel rejoiced that her steps had been arrested before the hour was too late. Letty, you *will* feel glad when you have time to think of this more calmly."

"You have heard your sister speak of her past love for Herbert Vaughan. It was an infatuation, a madness, irreconcilable with the passion of these latter days. I cannot drive my love out of my heart because he is unworthy of it—I have loved him too long and truly to do that ! "

"But——"

"Mr. Gear, I will hear no more. He is the craftiest of villains ; he is a coward, who has be-grudged a woman's life, and plotted to destroy it, but—I love him still ! "

"This is incomprehensible ! "

"He is poor, humiliated, and alone in the world. He passes from his house to ruin, and there will be no friend to teach him how to begin life anew, with a heart purified and chastened by this trial. Forgive me—think the worst of me—but I must go ! "

"There is a spell upon you."

"I must go!" she whispered, in a low earnest tone, that thrilled me. "Whatever happens, I must go to him!"

With her hands clasped together she went slowly from the room towards the hall—like a woman whose brain had been turned by the misfortunes besetting her. Whether she were mad or sane at that time, I have ever doubted—it has been beyond my power to solve.

I looked round. They had not noticed her departure; they were talking earnestly to Janet still —my mother had left her place, and joined them with my child in her arms—Joseph alone was glinting at me from the corners of his eyes. I followed Letty, whom I found with her hand on the lock of the great outer door.

"Pardon me, Miss Ray—but where are you going?"

"To him."

"This is sheer madness."

"I cannot help it—I am called thither—there is no power to stop me—there is no one here who has the right to say me nay."

"I have the moral right, at least."

"No!" she cried, impetuously.

"You are going to your fate—to shame—to ruin!"

"Do you not know me better than that?" she cried haughtily. "Have I ever proved myself so weak and erring as to be led to shame at this hour? No, Mr. Gear, I am going to help him —to be his friend—to follow his fortunes—to be ever at his side—to bid him be strong and resist temptation, when the evil hour comes back to him. Alone in the world, he will fall—with me, I see a brighter and a better life for him."

"Stay and reflect awhile—why this haste?"

"I saw an awful purpose in his face—he will go back to that house, conscious that all hope is past with him, and then—oh, my God!—the razor flashing in his hands. Mr. Gear, I must go!"

She flung back the door with a noise that shook the house—she went bare-headed, and like a madwoman, in the rain. At the last step she paused, and looked back at me.

"I said that I would love him all my life—God be my witness to that promise still. Mr. Gear, don't follow me—surely I possess the right to seek my own fate. Like him, I am friendless and alone."

"Miss Ray, I beg you to pause. I warn you that no good can follow this."

"I am past all warning—I am resolved."

"God help you, then!"

She went on through the rain, and I watched her hurry along the carriage-drive, drawn by the spell which bound her to that man, and which no revelation of his utter baseness could affect. At the great swing gate she turned and looked back at me—it was the face of a despairing woman that was turned to me. It shaped my course of action —it led me, at all risks, to attempt to stay her progress.

I snatched at my hat from the tree in the hall, and went out after her—she detected the movement, and fled on down the country-road.

I followed down the steps, feeling conscious, for the first time, that my strength was not what it had been—that the past excitement, the long sleepless hours, had rendered me very weak at last.

Half-way down the drive my brother Joseph joined me.

"Where are you going?"

"To stop Letty. She is going to her fate."

"Let her go—she is a fool. I always hated that woman."

"She is worth a hundred Herbert Vaughans— a generous and unselfish woman, whom I will not see sacrificed."

"As you will. Let us go on together, then."

"I will enter the house, and take her from his arms, if he dare to claim her as his friend. If he brave me at the last, I will not spare him even now."

"I never intended to spare him," said Joseph, drily.

"What do you mean?"

"We shall see."

CHAPTER XII.

DIEU DISPOSE.

LETTY ran on through the rain at a pace there
was no overtaking.   By no earthly means was it
possible to intercept her progress before she reached
Nettlewood House.

I gave up the attempt to pursue her, but continued my way, walking as rapidly as my
strength would allow, and outwalking Joseph even
in that weakness which I felt was gaining ground
upon me.

"Joseph, there is a long illness before me,"
I said.

"I hope not, Canute," he said, earnestly.   "I

think that this is only the fatigue occasioned by your journey."

"No—I shall be ill."

"What do you come out in the rain for?"

"To save that girl, worthy of a better fate."

"You think of entering the house—at once?"

"I must."

"There's no occasion—he cannot escape—there are officers watching him, and waiting my direction. I have arranged all."

"That man must go free—if it be Ellen's wish."

"The laws cannot be outraged," said my brother; "he has committed a great crime, and Ellen will be compelled to prosecute."

"This shall not be," .

"Eh?"

Joseph ever disliked my firmness, and was impressed by it.

"I say that this shall not be! Let him go his way, as Ellen wished, but let us save that girl from the consequences of her own mad act. He will resign her, I think."

"I will compel him," said Joseph; "unless he resign her, and by some means or other pay me the debt he owes me, I will not spare him. I have not schemed all this while to be robbed of my money as well as foiled of my revenge."

"He has not the money."

"He will procure it—he shall. If she be so fond of this man, she will write me a cheque to save him."

"No—I will not have that!"

"Well, well," adopting a conciliatory tone, "leave it to me. I will call on him at once."

We were close on Nettlewood House—Letty Ray had long since passed through the gates towards it. As we approached, a man's head appeared over the fence that divided the lower ground from the lake.

"I thought it was you, sir."

"Where is he?"

"In the house—a lady has just run in, I think to put him on his guard."

"Who is in the house?"

"One servant—he is in our pay, and keeps a watch upon him for us. Say the word as soon as you like, sir,—it is very cold work out here in the rain."

"I am going into the house—if the servant opens the street door, come at once."

"All right, sir."

"I accompany you," I said to my brother; "I will have no treachery. Together, or I go alone."

Joseph hesitated—and twitched his ear nervously.

"I suppose you must," he said, with a sigh, "but upon my soul, it is uncommonly hard, after all my trouble. Canute, you will not try to balk me out of my just rights?"

"No—but we must not *sell* that man his liberty."

"As quick as you can, sir," suggested the man, shuddering violently. "I don't like this part of the world at all. It gives me the horrors."

"How is that?" I asked.

"It rains so awfully hard that the very ground shakes under your feet. There now!"

I clutched the arm of my brother, for the earth vibrated—*shuddered*.

"Did you feel that?—or am I worse in health than I believe?"

"It is strange," said Joseph, thoughtfully. "It could not be fancy, and they don't have earthquakes in Cumberland."

A man, bare-headed, came running from the house—when he saw us he flung up his arms in horror. The man on watch leaped over the fence with an oath.

"I can't stop here—there's something awful coming."

"I must have my money," said Joseph.

"Back!—back for your life!" I shouted. "*The world is at an end!* My God! Look at the mountain!"

It was coming towards us! The great mountain behind the house at Nettlewood was sliding forward—the house was slowly moving on—the land shook, as with an earthquake—there was a crashing of trees, a noise of falling stones, and then the whole scene changed, and suddenly and awfully the house rocked and collapsed.

We stood horror-stricken, gazing at this scene; it was not to be realized on the instant, but to seem part of a wild dream for many a long day. Nettlewood House had gone forward with the landslip, and then broken up for ever.

*   *   *   *   *

I knew no more for many weeks. The illness that had been threatening me so long, came upon me then, and my brother and the two men carried me back to Miss Ray's house, a helpless infant, without power to move a limb.

When I was well enough to be conscious of the care that had been taken of me—to know the face of the dear faithful wife who had never left me during my long illness—of my sister's and mother's, of Joseph's—strangely altered, and full of a new earnestness—they spoke to me, cautiously at first, of the landslip that had brought half the geologists in the world to Nettlewood. Of the theories respecting it they told me nothing; or of the prophecies that one learned man had made years ago respecting that particular substratum on which the mountain was based—or of the convictions of many that the incessant rains had sapped at the spongy base until it had given way and brought the mountain shelving to the lake. They spoke only of the search for the two victims to the catastrophe—of their discovery, and burial in Henlock Churchyard—of the strange end to those two lives—a life of cautious crime, which spared no one in its course—and a life shadowed by a passion that turned to madness, and drove its victim to her death. A deep and earnest passion for an object utterly unworthy of it—one of those strange idolatries which shock the world of simple and pure-minded people, and are so hard to understand.

Poor Ellen understood it—for she had experienced the strange power which this Herbert Vaughan could exercise over women—she had suffered, and been scathed by it. *Her* ransom came too late for happiness.

Oh! for a less number of poor suffering women hurrying to their fate by spells incomprehensible to us! The temptation a mystery, but the sad result staring us in the face with each week's news, and shocking us in our streets by the sin and sorrow ever flitting by.

Letty's passion was akin to this—but not this! Let us leave it in its incomprehensibility, and dwell for a short while on the fortune she had left behind her—the fortune which had been schemed for, struggled for so long.

Letty Ray had left a will behind her, bequeathing her property to Herbert Vaughan. He had been her one thought all her life—she had feared for that life before leaving London, and executed a will, leaving Zitman's money to her lover—failing him, before her marriage, to Mary Gear, late Mary Zitman, of Nettlewood House.

So the money came round again by a strange chance; but it was money which we were superstitious concerning—which we put by for our children's future, and cared not to touch ourselves—which seemed to us ever shadowed by the darkest of reminiscences.

When our children grow up and require starting in the world, we may think of Letty Ray's fortune—when Edmund Wenford, a nervous invalid still, but a man strangely altered and subdued, requires assistance to begin life anew, we may draw upon it—when any of us are in want, or Ellen needs a wedding dowry—she is a grave-faced woman, who will never marry again, I fear—when there is distress in the land, and we feel that we have the power to assist the helpless.

We are happy in our quiet way—the partnership with Mr. Sanderson is a success—children cluster round our knees, and there is a true love in, our midst, that hallows home, and renders it a resting-place worth seeking from the world.

My mother and Ellen are living near us still—Joseph has opened business in London, and is a better and less covetous man—Janet is with us, our children's nurse and faithful friend. She has learned to love those children as she loved Mary and her brother in the times before the troubles came.

THE END.

LONDON : PRINTED BY MACDONALD AND TUGWELL, BLENHEIM HOUSE,

MESSRS. HURST AND BLACKETT'S
NEW PUBLICATIONS.

TRAVELS ON HORSEBACK IN MANTCHU

TARTARY : being a Summer's Ride beyond the GREAT WALL OF CHINA. By GEORGE FLEMING. 1 vol., royal 8vo., with Map and 50 Illustrations.

"Mr. Fleming's narrative is a most charming one. He has an untrodden region to tell of, and he photographs it and its people and their ways. Life-like descriptions are interspersed with personal anecdotes, local legends, and stories of adventure, some of them revealing no common artistic power."—*Spectator*.

"A more interesting book of travels has not been published for some time past than this. A new world has in fact been opened up by the adventurous spirit of the traveller. Canton and the southern districts of China have afforded abundant materials for works of travel; but of the far north, and the people that swarm beyond the Great Wall, nothing of a truthful character was hitherto known. The descriptions given by Mr. Fleming of the Great Wall, of Moukden—the Mantchu capital—and of the habits and occupations of the people, make an exceedingly interesting and highly instructive book."—*Observer*.

"Mr. Fleming has many of the best qualities of the traveller—good spirits, an excellent temper, sound sense, the faculty of observation, and a literary culture which has enlarged his sympathies with men and things. He has rendered us his debtor for much instruction and amusement. The value of his book is greatly enhanced by the illustrations, as graphic as copious and well executed, which is saying much."—*Reader*.

A PERSONAL NARRATIVE OF THIRTEEN

YEARS' SERVICE AMONGST THE WILD TRIBES OF KHONDISTAN, FOR THE SUPPRESSION OF HUMAN SACRIFICE. By Major-General JOHN CAMPBELL, C.B. 1 vol., 8vo., with Illustrations, 14s.

COURT AND SOCIETY FROM ELIZABETH

TO ANNE, Illustrated from the Papers at Kimbolton. By the DUKE OF MANCHESTER. 2 vols. 8vo, with Fine Portraits. (Just ready.)

ADVENTURES AND RESEARCHES among the

ANDAMAN ISLANDERS. By DR. MOUAT, F.R.G.S., &c. 1 vol., demy 8vo., with Illustrations. 16s.

"Dr. Mouat's book, whilst forming a most important and valuable contribution to ethnology, will be read with interest by the general reader."—*Athenæum*.

"Dr. Mouat's volume will be welcome to very many by reason of the strange information with which it abounds. It is both amusing and instructive."—*Examiner*.

THE LIFE OF EDWARD IRVING, Minister of

the National Scotch Church, London. Illustrated by HIS JOURNAL AND CORRESPONDENCE. By Mrs. OLIPHANT. SECOND EDITION, REVISED. 2 vols. 8vo, with Portrait.

"We who read these memoirs must own to the nobility of Irving's character, the grandeur of his aims, and the extent of his powers. His friend Carlyle bears this testimony to his worth:—'I call him, on the whole, the best man I have ever, after trial enough, found in this world, or hope to find.' A character such as this is deserving of study, and his life ought to be written. Mrs. Oliphant has undertaken the work, and has produced a biography of considerable merit. The author fully understands her hero, and sets forth the incidents of his career with the skill of a practised hand. The book is a good book on a most interesting theme."—*Times*.

"Mrs. Oliphant's 'Life of Edward Irving' supplies a long-felt desideratum. It is copious, earnest, and eloquent. On every page there is the impress of a large and masterly comprehension, and of a bold, fluent, and poetic skill of portraiture. Irving as a man and as a pastor is not only fully sketched, but exhibited with many powerful and life-like touches, which leave a strong impression."—*Edinburgh Review*.

"A truly interesting and most affecting memoir. Irving's life ought to have a niche in every gallery of religious biography. There are few lives that will be fuller of instruction, interest, and consolation."—*Saturday Review*.

MESSRS. HURST AND BLACKETT'S
NEW WORKS—*Continued.*

MEMOIRS OF JANE CAMERON, FEMALE
CONVICT. By a PRISON MATRON, Author of "Female Life in Prison." 2 vols., 21s.

THE DESTINY OF THE NATIONS, AS INDI-
CATED IN PROPHECY. By the Rev. JOHN CUMMING, D.D. 1 vol. 7s. 6d. (Just ready.)

THE LAST DECADE OF A GLORIOUS REIGN;
completing "THE HISTORY OF HENRY IV,. King of France and Navarre," from Original and Authentic Sources. By M. W. FREER. 2 vols., with Portraits. 21s.

"The best and most comprehensive work on the reign of Henry IV. available to English readers. The Court History of Henry's Glorious Reign can hardly be more completely told than Miss Freer has told it."—*Examiner.*

"These volumes are as creditable to the judgment as they are to the zeal and industry of the author."—*Athenæum.*

LES MISÉRABLES. By VICTOR HUGO. THE
AUTHORIZED COPYRIGHT ENGLISH TRANSLATION. THIRD EDITION. Complete in 3 vols. post 8vo. Price 31s. 6d.

"We think it will be seen on the whole that this work has something more than the beauties of an exquisite style or the word compelling power of a literary Zeus to recommend it to the tender care of a distant posterity; that in dealing with all the emotions, passions, doubts, fears, which go to make up our common humanity, M. Victor Hugo has stamped upon every page the hall-mark of genius and the loving patience and conscientious labour of a true artist. But the merits of Les Misérables do not merely consist in the conception of it as a whole, it abounds page after page with details of unequalled beauty."—*Quarterly Review.*

" 'Les Misérables' is one of those rare works which have a strong personal interest in addition to their intrinsic importance. It is not merely the work of a truly great man, but it is his great and favourite work—the fruit of years of thought and labour. Victor Hugo is almost the only French imaginative writer of the present century who is entitled to be considered as a man of genius He has wonderful poetical power, and he has the faculty, which hardly any other French novelist possesses, of drawing beautiful as well as striking pictures. Another feature for which Victor Hugo's book deserves high praise is its perfect purity. Any one who reads the Bible and Shakspeare may read 'Les Misérables.' The story is admirable, and is put together with unsurpassable art, care, life, and simplicity. Some of the characters are drawn with consummate skill."—*Daily News.*

ITALY UNDER VICTOR EMMANUEL. A
Personal Narrative. By COUNT CHARLES ARRIVABENE. 2 v., 8vo.

"Whoever wishes to gain an insight into the Italy of the present moment, and to know what she is, what she has done, and what she has to do, should consult Count Arrivabene's ample volumes, which are written in a style singularly vivid and dramatic."—*Dickens's All the Year Round.*

HISTORY OF ENGLAND, FROM THE
ACCESSION OF JAMES I. TO THE DISGRACE OF CHIEF JUSTICE COKE. By SAMUEL RAWSON GARDINER, late Student of Christchurch. 2 vols. 8vo. 30s.

"We thank Mr. Gardiner much for his able, intelligent, and interesting book. We will not do him the injustice to say it is the best history of the period which it covers: it is the only history."—*Spectator.*

THE PRIVATE DIARY OF RICHARD, DUKE
OF BUCKINGHAM AND CHANDOS, K.G. 3 vols.

MESSRS. HURST AND BLACKETT'S
NEW WORKS—*Continued.*

A LADY'S VISIT TO MANILLA & JAPAN.
By ANNA D'A. 1 vol., with Illustration, 14s.

"This book is written in a lively, agreeable, natural style, and we cordially recommend it as containing a fund of varied information connected with the Far East, not to be found recorded in so agreeable a manner in any other volume with which we are acquainted."—*Press.*

"The author has given a picturesque and animated account of her voyages, and of the most noteworthy objects which presented themselves in the course of her progress from Singapore to China, and thence to Manilla and Japan."—*Post.*

THE WANDERER IN WESTERN FRANCE.
By G. T. LOWTH, Esq., Author of "The Wanderer in Arabia." Illustrated by the HON. ELIOT YORKE, M.P. 8vo. 15s.

"Mr. Lowth reminds us agreeably of Washington Irving."—*Athenæum.*

"If Mr. Lowth's conversation is only half as good as his book, he must be a very charming acquaintance. The art of gossiping in his style, never wearying the listener, yet perpetually conveying to him valuable information, is a very rare one, and he possesses it in perfection. No one will quit his volume without feeling that he understands Brittany and La Vendée."—*Spectator.*

A WINTER IN UPPER AND LOWER EGYPT.
By G. A. HOSKINS, Esq., F.R.G.S. 1 vol., with Illustrations, 15s.

"As a contribution to geography, Mr. Hoskins's work is a most excellent one. In his archæological researches he is as entertaining a guide as Belzoni himself, and the ancient mythology of the country is treated by him with a breadth and scope of intellect worthy of a Bunsen; whilst his description of the journey up the Nile is as charming as Moore's account of the voyage of the Epicurean upon the same historic stream."—*Observer.*

"To travellers recommended to explore the Nile in search of health this volume will be invaluable. It abounds with excellent practical advice and instruction—an advantage which renders it superior to all other Egyptian works of travel we have met with."—*Sun.*

GREECE AND THE GREEKS. Being the
Narrative of a Winter Residence and Summer Travel in Greece and its Islands. By FREDRIKA BREMER. Translated by MARY HOWITT. 2 vols., 21s.

"The best book of travels which this charming authoress has given to the public."—*Athenæum.*

POINTS OF CONTACT BETWEEN SCIENCE
AND ART. By His Eminence CARDINAL WISEMAN. 8vo. 5s.

"Cardinal Wiseman's interesting work contains suggestions of real value. It is divided into three heads, treating respectively of painting, sculpture, and architecture. The cardinal handles his subject in a most agreeable manner."—*Art Journal.*

HEROES, PHILOSOPHERS, AND COURTIERS
of the TIME of LOUIS XVI. 2 vols. 21s.

"This work is full of amusing and interesting anecdote, and supplies many links in the great chain of events of a most remarkable period.—*Examiner.*

MEMOIRS OF CHRISTINA, QUEEN OF
SWEDEN. By HENRY WOODHEAD. 2 vols. with Portrait, 21s.

"An impartial history of the life of Queen Christina and portraiture of her character are placed before the public in these valuable and interesting volumes."—*Press.*

LIFE AMONG CONVICTS. By the Rev. C. B.
GIBSON, M.R.I.A., Chaplain in the Convict Service. 2 vols. 21s.

"All concerned in that momentous question—the treatment of our convicts—may peruse with interest and benefit the very valuable information laid before them by Mr. Gibson in the most pleasant and lucid manner possible."—*Sun.*

MESSRS. HURST AND BLACKETT'S
NEW WORKS—*Continued.*

ENGLISH WOMEN OF LETTERS. By JULIA
KAVANAGH, Author of "Nathalie," "Adéle," "French Women of
Letters," "Queen Mab," &c. 2 vols., 21s.

"This work of Miss Kavanagh's will be a pleasant contribution to the literature of
the times, and in raising a shrine to the merits of some of the leading English women of
literature, Miss Kavanagh has also associated her own name with theirs. The work
comprises a biography of each authoress (all women of renown in their day and generation), and an account and analysis of her principal novels. To this task Miss Kavanagh
has brought knowledge of her subject, delicacy of discrimination, industry, and a genial
humour, which makes her sketches pleasant to read."—*Athenæum.*

MAN; OR, THE OLD AND NEW PHILOSOPHY:
Being Notes and Facts for the Curious, with especial reference to
recent writers on the subject of the Antiquity of Man. By the
Rev. B. W. SAVILE, M.A.. 1 vol., 10s. 6d.

DRIFTWOOD, SEAWEED, AND FALLEN
LEAVES. By the Rev. JOHN CUMMING, D.D. 2 vols., 21s.

" In these volumes the social, literary, moral, and religious questions of the day are
treated with much clearness of perception and great liberality of sentiment."—*Observer.*

THE LIFE OF J. M. W. TURNER, R.A., from
Original Letters and Papers furnished by his Friends, and
Fellow Academicians. By WALTER THORNBURY. 2 vols. 8vo.
with Portraits and other Illustrations.

TRAVELS IN BRITISH COLUMBIA; with the
Narrative of a Yacht Voyage Round Vancouver's Island. By
Captain C. E. BARRETT LENNARD. 1 vol. 8vo.

THE CHURCH AND THE CHURCHES; or,
THE PAPACY AND THE TEMPORAL POWER. By Dr.
DÖLLINGER. Translated, by W. B. MAC CABE. 8vo.

FEMALE LIFE IN PRISON. By a PRISON MA-
TRON. THIRD EDITION, WITH ADDITIONS. 2 vols., 21s.

" There are many obvious reasons why records of prison life should prove an attractive department of literature. The present volumes have at least this higher pretension,
that while they satiate our interest in pet murderesses and other prison monstrosities,
they aim at affording us a fuller view of the working of a retired and special department of State administration. The authoress, who has herself been a prison matron,
writes throughout with good sense, good taste, and good feeling. The phenomena of
female prison life which she describes are most curious, and we consider her book to be
as authentic as it is new in the form and details of its information."—*The Times.*

THE OKAVANGO RIVER; A NARRATIVE OF
TRAVEL, EXPLORATION, AND ADVENTURE. By
CHARLES JOHN ANDERSSON, Author of "Lake Ngami." 1 vol.,
with Portrait and numerous Illustrations.

TRAVELS IN THE REGIONS OF THE
AMOOR, AND THE RUSSIAN ACQUISITIONS ON THE CONFINES OF
INDIA AND CHINA. By T. W. ATKINSON, F.G.S., F.R.G.S.,
Author of "Oriental and Western Siberia." Dedicated, by per-
mission, to HER MAJESTY. Second Edition. Royal 8vo., with
Map and 83 Illustrations. Elegantly bound.

THIRTY YEARS' MUSICAL RECOLLEC-
TIONS. By HENRY F. CHORLEY. 2 vols., with Portraits.

Published annually, in One Vol., royal 8vo, with the Arms beautifully engraved, handsomely bound, with gilt edges, price 31s. 6d.

LODGE'S PEERAGE
AND BARONETAGE,
CORRECTED BY THE NOBILITY.

THE THIRTY-SECOND EDITION FOR 1863 IS NOW READY.

LODGE'S PEERAGE AND BARONETAGE is acknowledged to be the most complete, as well as the most elegant, work of the kind. As an established and authentic authority on all questions respecting the family histories, honours, and connections of the titled aristocracy, no work has ever stood so high. It is published under the especial patronage of Her Majesty, and is annually corrected throughout, from the personal communications of the Nobility. It is the only work of its class in which, *the type being kept constantly standing*, every correction is made in its proper place to the date of publication, an advantage which gives it supremacy over all its competitors. Independently of its full and authentic information respecting the existing Peers and Baronets of the realm, the most sedulous attention is given in its pages to the collateral branches of the various noble families, and the names of many thousand individuals are introduced, which do not appear in other records of the titled classes. For its authority, correctness, and facility of arrangement, and the beauty of its typography and binding, the work is justly entitled to the place it occupies on the tables of Her Majesty and the Nobility.

LIST OF THE PRINCIPAL CONTENTS.

Historical View of the Peerage.
Parliamentary Roll of the House of Lords.
English, Scotch, and Irish Peers, in their orders of Precedence.
Alphabetical List of Peers of Great Britain and the United Kingdom, holding superior rank in the Scotch or Irish Peerage.
Alphabetical List of Scotch and Irish Peers, ho'ding superior titles in the Peerage of Great Britain and the United Kingdom.
A Collective List of Peers, in their order of Precedence.
Table of Precedency among Men.
Table of Precedency among Women.
The Queen and the Royal Family.
Peers of the Blood Royal.
The Peerage, alphabetically arranged.
Families of such Extinct Peers as have left Widows or Issue.
Alphabetical List of the Surnames of all the Peers.

The Archbishops and Bishops of England, Ireland, and the Colonies.
The Baronetage, alphabetically arranged.
Alphabetical List of Surnames assumed by members of Noble Families.
Alphabetical List of the Second Titles of Peers, usually borne by their Eldest Sons.
Alphabetical Index to the Daughters of Dukes, Marquises, and Earls, who, having married Commoners, retain the title of Lady before their own Christian and their Husbands' Surnames.
Alphabetical Index to the Daughters of Viscounts and Barons, who, having married Commoners, are styled Honourable Mrs.; and, in case of the husband being a Baronet or Knight, Honourable Lady.
Mottoes alphabetically arranged and translated.

" Lodge's Peerage must supersede all other works of the kind, for two reasons; first it is on a better plan; and secondly, it is better executed. We can safely pronounce it to be the readiest, the most useful, and exactest of modern works on the subject."—*Spectator*.
" A work which corrects all errors of former works. It is a most useful publication."—*Times*.
" As perfect a Peerage as we are ever likely to see published."—*Herald*.

𝕳𝖚𝖗𝖘𝖙 𝖆𝖓𝖉 𝕭𝖑𝖆𝖈𝖐𝖊𝖙𝖙'𝖘 𝕾𝖙𝖆𝖓𝖉𝖆𝖗𝖉 𝕷𝖎𝖇𝖗𝖆𝖗𝖞
(CONTINUED).

VOL. XIII.—DARIEN. BY ELIOT WARBURTON.
"This last production, from the pen of the author of 'The Crescent and the Cross,' has the same elements of a very wide popularity. It will please its thousands."—*Globe.*

VOL. XIV.—FAMILY ROMANCE; OR, DOMESTIC ANNALS OF THE ARISTOCRACY.
BY SIR BERNARD BURKE.
"It were impossible to praise too highly as a work of amusement this most interesting book. It ought to be found on every drawing-room table."—*Standard.*

VOL. XV.—THE LAIRD OF NORLAW.
BY THE AUTHOR OF "MRS. MARGARET MAITLAND."
"Scottish life and character are here delineated with true artistic skill."—*Herald.*

VOL. XVI.—THE ENGLISHWOMAN IN ITALY.
"Mrs. Gretton's work is interesting, and full of instruction."—*The Times.*

VOL. XVII.—NOTHING NEW.
BY THE AUTHOR OF "JOHN HALIFAX, GENTLEMAN."
"We cordially commend this book. The same graphic power, deep pathos, healthful sentiment, and masterly execution, which place that beautiful work 'John Halifax,' among the English classics, are everywhere displayed."—*Chronicle.*

VOL. XVIII.—THE LIFE OF JEANNE D'ALBRET.
"Nothing can be more interesting than Miss Freer's story of the life of Jeanne d'Albret, and the narrative is as trustworthy as it is attractive."—*Post.*

VOL. XIX.—THE VALLEY OF A HUNDRED FIRES.
BY THE AUTHOR OF "MARGARET AND HER BRIDESMAIDS."
"If asked to classify this work, we should give it a place between 'John Halifax,' and 'The Caxtons.'"—*Herald.*

VOL. XX.—THE ROMANCE OF THE FORUM.
BY PETER BURKE, SERJEANT AT LAW.
"A work of singular interest, which can never fail to charm. The present cheap and elegant edition includes the true story of the Colleen Bawn."—*Illustrated News.*

VOL. XXI.—ADELE. BY JULIA KAVANAGH.
"Adèle is the best work we have had by Miss Kavanagh; it is a charming story. The interest kindled in the first chapter burns brightly to the close."—*Athenæum.*

VOL. XXII. STUDIES FROM LIFE.
BY THE AUTHOR OF "JOHN HALIFAX, GENTLEMAN."
"These 'Studies from Life' are remarkable for graphic power and observation. The book will not diminish the reputation of the accomplished author."—*Saturday Review.*

VOL. XXIII.—GRANDMOTHER'S MONEY.
"A good novel. The most interesting of the author's productions."—*Athenæum.*

VOL. XXIV.—A BOOK ABOUT DOCTORS.
BY J. C. JEAFFRESON ESQ.
"A delightful book."—*Athenæum.* 'A book to be read and re-read; fit for the study as well as the drawing-room table and the circulating library."—*Lancet.*

VOL. XXV.—NO CHURCH.
"We advise all who have the opportunity to read this book. It is well worth the study."—*Athenæum*

VOL. XXVI.—MISTRESS AND MAID.
BY THE AUTHOR OF "JOHN HALIFAX, GENTLEMAN."
"A good, wholesome book, gracefully written, and as pleasant to read as it is instructive."—*Athenæum.*

THE NEW AND POPULAR NOVELS,
PUBLISHED BY HURST & BLACKETT.

QUEEN MAB. By JULIA KAVANAGH, Author of
"Nathalie," "Adèle," &c. 3 vols.

"This is one of the best productions of Miss Kavanagh's pen. Queen Mab is more charming than any other former creation. The story will find much favour with the public."—*Observer.*

THE BROWNS AND THE SMITHS. By the
Author of "Anne Dysart," &c. 2 vols.

THE WIFE'S EVIDENCE. By W. G. WILLS, Esq.,
Author of "Notice to Quit," &c. 3 vols.

GOOD SOCIETY. By Mrs. GREY, Author of
"The Gambler's Wife," &c. 3 vols.

"'Good Society,' in all its various phases, comes in for a complete anatomisation at the hands of our author. That very many of the characters are sketched from life can admit of no doubt. The dialogue is lively, and the 'interiors' are painted with a well accustomed hand, whether the scene is laid in the marquis's mansion, the squire's hall, the country parsonage, the Romish chapel, or the lodging-house in Belgravia. Altogether, to our mind, this surpasses any of the former works of the writer."—*United Service Magazine.* "Mrs. Grey writes well, and with spirit."—*Post.*

MARY LYNDSAY. By LADY EMILY PONSONBY.

"The best-written and most interesting of the author's works."—*Post.*
"An original and graceful story. The character of Mary Lyndsay is most beautifully and nobly conceived."—*John Bull.*

BARBARA'S HISTORY. By AMELIA B. EDWARDS.
Author of "My Brother's Wife," &c. 3 vols

LOST AND SAVED. By THE HON. MRS. NORTON.
Fourth Edition. With a Letter from the Author. 8 vols.

LEFT TO THEMSELVES. By the Author of
"Cousin Geoffrey," &c. 3 vols.

"A very graphic, forcible, and interesting work."—*Sun.*

FLORIAN'S HUSBAND. 3 vols.

"A brilliant work, beautifully written."—*Sun.*

CHURCH AND CHAPEL. By the Author of "High
Church," "No Church," and "Owen: a Waif." 3 vols.

"This novel sustains the credit of the author's previous works. It is a story of well-sustained interest."—*Athenæum.*

VERONIA. 3 vols.

"This novel exhibits no mean powers of conception and expression."—*Post.*

RESPECTABLE SINNERS. By MRS. BROTHER-
TON, Author of "Arthur Brandon." 3 vols.

LIVE IT DOWN. By J. C. JEAFFRESON, Third
Edition. Revised. 3 vols.

"This story will satisfy most readers. The interest goes on increasing to the last page. It is by far the best work of fiction Mr. Jeaffreson has written."—*Athenæum.*

HEART AND CROSS. By the Author of "Mar-
garet Maitland." 1 vol.

"A delightful work. The interest is preserved to the closing page."—*Post.*

THREE LIVES IN ONE. 3 vols.

"This story abounds with life and character."—*Sun.*

VICISSITUDES OF A GENTLEWOMAN. 3 v.